Overcoming Paranoid & Suspicious Thoughts

A Self-help Guide Using Cognitive Behavioral Techniques

Daniel Freeman

Jason Freeman

Philippa Garety

16

EasyRead Large

Copyright Page from the Original Book

Constable & Robinson Ltd
3 The Lanchesters
162 Fulham Palace Road
London W6 9ER
www.constablerobinson.com

First published in the UK by Robinson,
an imprint of Constable & Robinson Ltd 2006

Important Note
This book is not intended as a substitute for medical advice or treatment.
Any person with a condition requiring medical attention should consult a
qualified medical practitioner or suitable therapist.

A copy of the British Library Cataloguing in
Publication Data is available from the British Library.

ISBN: 978-1-84529-219-5

3 5 7 9 10 8 6 4

Printed and bound in the EU

TABLE OF CONTENTS

DR DANIEL FREEMAN is a Wellcome Trust Fellow and Senior Lecturer in Clinical Psychology at King's College London and an Honorary Consultant Clinical Psychologist in the South London and Maudsley NHS Foundation Trust. **PROFESSOR PHILIPPA GARETY** is Professor of Clinical Psychology at College, London and Head of Psychology in the South London and Maudsley NHS Foundation Trust. Both are internationally renowned researchers based at the Institute of Psychiatry, London as well as practising clinical psychologists specializing in the treatment of persecutory thoughts. **JASON FREEMAN** is an experienced writer and has spent ten years working as an editor in academic publishing.

The authors offer further accounts of suspicious thoughts, details of their research and the opportunity to provide feedback on this book at www.paranoidthoughts.com

Praise for Overcoming Paranoid and Suspicious Thoughts

'Everybody is upset from time to time by suspicious thoughts regarding other people's motives. For the first time, the problem of the exaggerated fear of being harmed is laid out in detail. In a clear, engaging style, the authors trace the origins of these fears and tell us what to do about them. This book is essential reading for the large number of people who are plagued by suspicions of other people.'

Aaron T. Beck, University Professor of Psychiatry, University of Pennsylvania and President of the Beck Institute for Cognitive Therapy and Research, USA.

'Although fears and suspicions about others are extremely common and a source of great suffering and social conflict, no book has ever been published to help people deal with such problems. Now finally a group of the world's foremost scientists in the field have come up with a very accessible and readable text providing solutions for those who previously had no source to access.'

Jim van Os, Professor of Psychiatry and Head of University Psychiatric Clinic, Maastricht University Hospital, The Netherlands

'Until recently the problems caused by suspicious thoughts were greatly underestimated. We had little idea that they were so common, no real sense of what caused them, and no clear strategy for how to tackle them. The authors of this excellent and timely book have played a major role in developing our understanding of how suspicious thoughts arise and, crucially, how we can learn to cope with them. *Overcoming Paranoid and Suspicious Thoughts* is a first-class distillation of their ground-breaking research that will surely establish itself as the best self-help guide on the subject for many years to come.'

Nicholas Tarrier, Professor of Clinical Psychology, Manchester University and Consultant

Clinical Psychologist, Manchester Mental Health and Social Care NHS Trust.

'Many of us harbour paranoid and suspicious ideas that have no basis in fact, but it's not something we tend to talk about. This pioneering book shows that, just as many of us can have mild anxiety or depressed feelings without ever requiring specialist help, many of us have minor (but troubling) paranoid thoughts. Most importantly, the book proposes simple and practical ways to understand and overcome these ideas.'

Robin Murray, Professor of Psychiatry, King's College London, and Head of the National Psychosis Unit, South London and Maudsley NHS Trust.

'Suspiciousness and irrational fears of being harmed by others are common and distressing experiences, but often go unrecognized. This book is the first to offer practical help to people suffering from this type of difficulty. It is written in a warm and engaging style, aimed at the non-specialist. It will be enormously helpful both to people suffering from suspiciousness and paranoia, and to their friends and relatives.'

Richard Bentall, Professor of Experimental Clinical Psychology and Consultant Clinical Psychologist, Manchester University.

'Feeling depressed, anxious or having an urge to recheck things are universal experiences; in fact they are helpful emotions that motivate us to face up to the day to day problems that life throws at us. But they can often escalate and we become aware that they have become our masters and need to be reined in. Suspiciousness is likewise a normal emotion that can serve us well; but overuse it and we can lose the capacity to trust people and soon we are on a slippery slope to isolation and despair. This book is a welcome addition to the self-help literature. It firmly places suspicious thinking in a normal context and offers straightforward, scientifically based guidance to the average man or woman in the street to understand it and to bring it back under control again.'

Max Birchwood, Professor of Mental Health, University of Birmingham and Director of Early Intervention Services Birmingham and Solihull Mental Health NHS Trust.

www.paranoidthoughts.com

The aim of the **Overcoming** series is to enable people with a range of common problems and disorders to take control of their own recovery program. Each title, with its specially tailored program, is devised by a practising clinician using the latest techniques of cognitive behavioral therapy – techniques which have been shown to be highly effective in changing the way people think about themselves and their problems. The series was initiated in 1993 by Peter Cooper, Professor of Psychology at Reading University and Research Fellow at the University of Cambridge in the UK, whose original volume on overcoming bulimia nervosa and binge-eating continues to help many people in the USA, the UK and Europe. Many of the books in the Overcoming series are recommended by the UK Department of Health under the Books on Prescription scheme.

Other titles in the series include:

OVERCOMING ANGER AND IRRITABILITY
OVERCOMING ANOREXIA NERVOSA
OVERCOMING ANXIETY
OVERCOMING BULIMIA NERVOSA AND BINGE-EATING
OVERCOMING CHILDHOOD TRAUMA
OVERCOMING CHRONIC FATIGUE
OVERCOMING CHRONIC PAIN
OVERCOMING COMPULSIVE GAMBLING
OVERCOMING DEPERSONALIZATION AND FEELINGS
OF UNREALITY

OVERCOMING DEPRESSION
OVERCOMING DEPRESSION: TALKS WITH YOUR
THERAPIST (AUDIO)
OVERCOMING GRIEF
OVERCOMING INSOMNIA AND SLEEP PROBLEMS
OVERCOMING LOW SELF-ESTEEM
OVERCOMING MOOD SWINGS
OVERCOMING OBSESSIVE COMPULSIVE DISORDER
OVERCOMING PANIC
OVERCOMING PROBLEM DRINKING
OVERCOMING RELATIONSHIP PROBLEMS
OVERCOMING SEXUAL PROBLEMS
OVERCOMING SOCIAL ANXIETY AND SHYNESS
OVERCOMING TRAUMATIC STRESS
OVERCOMING WEIGHT PROBLEMS
OVERCOMING YOUR SMOKING HABIT
OVERCOMING WORRY
OVERCOMING YOUR CHILD'S FEARS AND WORRIES
OVERCOMING YOUR CHILD'S SHYNESS AND SOCIAL
ANXIETY

All titles in the series are available by mail order.
Please see the order form at the back of this book.
www.overcoming.co.uk.

Acknowledgments

The past ten years have seen a transformation in the under-standing and treatment of suspiciousness and related problems. This book draws not only on our own work in the field, but also the insights of many other scientists and clinicians. We would particularly like to acknowledge our research group colleagues Elizabeth Kuipers, David Fowler, Paul Bebbington and Graham Dunn. Our team's work has been funded in particular by the Wellcome Trust, an independent charity supporting research to improve human and animal health.

Many of the ideas we discuss have also stemmed from the clinical research of influential clinical psychologists and psychiatrists working in UK National Health Service Trusts and UK university departments such as Richard Bentall, Max Birchwood, Christine Barrowclough, Paul Chadwick, David Clark, Gillian Haddock, David Hemsley, Peter Kinderman, David Kingdon, Anthony Morrison, Emmanuelle Peters, Paul Salkovskis, Nick Tarrier, Peter Trower and Douglas Turkington. Moreover, this research endeavour has been personally guided from the US by one of the founders of cognitive therapy: Aaron Beck.

The other main source for this book has been the clients we've seen in our clinical practice. Our ideas and treatment strategies have developed from an interaction between academic research and discussions with individuals about their own real-life experiences of suspicious thoughts.

Preface

This is the first self-help guide to dealing with suspicious thoughts – and it seems to us to arrive at just the right moment.

Fears about other people seem to have reached new heights, whether they be terrorists, binge-drinking youths, child abusers or criminals. And recent scientific research has revealed that suspiciousness is much more common than had previously been believed. If you're worried about other people you're certainly not alone: around a third of the population regularly has suspicious or paranoid thoughts. In fact, suspiciousness may be almost as common as depression or anxiety. But while the bookshops are full of books on those topics, there are none on suspicious thoughts.

We have realized that suspiciousness is not only common among the people we see at our clinics but also in the general population. At the same time, there have been huge leaps forward in the scientific research into paranoid and suspicious thoughts. We are now much better placed to understand why someone is having suspicious thoughts and why they can be so distressing. We also now have a really effective treatment for paranoid and suspicious thoughts: cognitive therapy. It is this treatment that we'll share with you over the course of this book.

Not only has suspiciousness been underestimated as an issue, it's also something people are reluctant to talk about. (Maybe that's partly *why* it's been underestimated.)

In the first half of this book we explain what suspicious thoughts are, how they come about and what it feels like to experience them. We want to bring this hidden problem right out into the open. We also believe that *understanding* a problem is an essential step toward conquering it. In the second half we build on this understanding to present six practical steps to help you cope with your fears. Throughout the book we use accounts of suspicious thoughts that are based on real-life examples from our clinical practice.

Work through the chapters one by one. You will come to understand your suspicious thoughts – and you'll learn to overcome them.

Daniel Freeman, Jason Freeman,
Philippa Garety

Introduction by Peter Cooper

Why a cognitive behavioral approach?

You may have picked up this book uncertain as to why a psychological approach, such as a cognitive behavioral one, might help you overcome your difficulties with paranoid thoughts and feelings. A brief account of the history of this form of treatment might be helpful and encouraging. In the 1950s and 1960s a set of therapeutic techniques was developed, collectively termed 'behavior therapy'. These techniques shared two basic features. First, they aimed to remove symptoms (such as anxiety) by dealing with those symptoms themselves, rather than their deep-seated under lying historical causes (traditionally the focus of psychoanalysis, the app roach developed by Sigmund Freud and his associates). Second, they were techniques loosely related to what laboratory psychologists were finding out about the mechanisms of learning, which could potentially be put to the test, or had already been proven to be of practical value to sufferers. The area where these techniques proved to be of most value was in the treatment of anxiety disorders, especially specific phobias (such as extreme fear of animals or heights) and agoraphobia, both notoriously difficult to treat using conventional psycho therapies.

After an initial flush of enthusiasm, discontent with behavior therapy grew. There were a number of reasons for this, an important one of which was the fact that behavior therapy did not deal with the internal thoughts which were so obviously central to the distress that many patients were experiencing. In particular, behavior therapy proved inadequate when it came to the treatment of depression. In the late 1960s and early 1970s a treatment for depression was developed called 'cognitive therapy'. The pioneer in this enterprise was an American psychiatrist, Professor Aaron T. Beck. He developed a theory of depression which emphasized the importance of people's depressed styles of thinking, and, on the basis of this theory, he specified a new form of therapy. It would not be an exaggeration to say that Beck's work has changed the nature of psychotherapy, not just for depression but for a range of psychological problems.

The techniques introduced by Beck have been merged with the techniques developed earlier by the behavior therapists to produce a therapeutic approach which has come to be known as 'cognitive behavioral therapy' (or CBT). This therapy has been subjected to the strictest scientific testing and it has been found to be a highly successful treatment for a significant proportion of cases of depression. It has now become clear that specific patterns of disturbed thinking are associated with a wide range of psychological problems, not just depression, and that the treatments which deal with these are highly effective. So, effective cognitive behavioral treatments have been developed for anxiety disorders, like panic disorder, generalized anxiety disorder, specific phobias, social phobia, obsessive compulsive disorders and hypochondriasis (health anxiety), as well as for other conditions such as compulsive gambling, drug addiction, and eating disorders like bulimia nervosa. Indeed, cognitive behavioral techniques have been found to have an application beyond the narrow categories of psychological disorders. They have been used effectively, for example, to help people give up smoking or deal with their drinking problems; they have been used to help couples with marital difficulties; and they have been used to help people who have problems with the way they think about others, such as those who suffer from extreme jealousy or, as in this book, those who have distressing thoughts that people are against them.

The starting-point for CBT is the realization that the way we think, feel and behave are all intimately linked, and that changing the way we think about ourselves, our experiences, and the world around us changes the way we feel and what we are able to do. So, for example, by helping a depressed person identify and challenge their automatic depressive thoughts, a route out of the cycle of distressing thoughts and feelings can be found. Similarly, by helping someone with paranoid thoughts become aware of the circumstances under which these thoughts arise and what steps they can take to forestall and control them, a route to a calmer and less threatened life can be found.

Although effective CBT treatments have been developed for a wide range of disorders and problems, these treatments are not widely available, and when people try to help themselves on their own they often do things which make matters worse. In recent years the community of cognitive behavioral therapists has responded to this situation by taking the principles and techniques of specific cognitive behavioral therapies for particular problems and presenting them in books which people can read and apply themselves. These manuals specify a systematic program of treatment which the individual works through to overcome their difficulties. In this way, cognitive behavioral techniques of proven value are being made available on the widest possible basis.

Self-help books are never going to replace therapists. Many people will need individual treatment from a qualified therapist. It is also the case that, despite the widespread success of cognitive behavioral therapy, some people will not respond to it and will need one of the other treatments available. Nevertheless, although research on the use of these self-help books is at an early stage, the work done to date indicates that for a great many people such a manual will prove sufficient for them to overcome their problems without professional help. Many people suffer silently and secretly for years. Sometimes appropriate help is not forthcoming despite their efforts to find it. Sometimes they feel too ashamed or guilty to reveal their problems to anyone. For many of these people the cognitive behavioral self-help books will provide a lifeline to recovery and a better future.

Professor Peter Cooper
The University of Reading, 2006

PART ONE

Understanding Suspicious Thoughts

1

What do we mean by 'suspicious thoughts about others'?

You go into a strange diner in the South and everything goes quiet, and you realize all the other customers are looking at you as if they are sizing up the risk involved in murdering you and leaving your body in a shallow grave somewhere out in the swamps.

Bill Bryson

Even a paranoid can have enemies.

Golda Meir

When I look back on all these worries, I remember the story of the old man who said on his deathbed that he had had a lot of trouble in his life, most of which had never happened.

Winston Churchill

Introduction

It sometimes seems as if the one thing that unites the diverse peoples of the world is our fear of one another. Worries about other people are so common that they seem to be an essential, if unwelcome, part of what it means to be human.

People from a different country, people who do not share our religious or political beliefs or our sexual orientation, even people with an unusual haircut or style of dress – all are frequently the objects of our distrust, anxiety or fear.

On a more mundane level, who hasn't worried about walking along a deserted street late at night? Who hasn't fretted, approaching home after a time away, that the house may have been burgled in their absence? Who hasn't found themselves suspecting, perhaps only for a moment, that a friend, colleague or family member hasn't their best interests at heart?

These anxieties may take many different forms and may vary hugely in degree, but what unites them is the suspicion that *other people intend to do us harm.* There is no doubt that these worries are extremely common among people of all ages, from adolescence to old age. In fact, suspicious and paranoid thoughts may well be as widespread as happy, angry, depressed or anxious thoughts. In one recent survey.

• 70 per cent of people said that they had, at some time, experienced the feeling that people were deliberately trying to harm or upset them in some way.

In another study:

• 93 per cent of respondents believed that, at some point, they had been talked about behind their back; and
• 80 per cent of people had often felt that strangers were looking at them critically.

It is rare to go through life without having a paranoid thought. But how many people get these thoughts frequently? We recently surveyed over a thousand people to see how many regularly had suspicious thoughts. Here are a couple of the major discoveries we made:

• 30–40 per cent of the people we surveyed thought once a week that negative comments about them were being put around.
• 10–30 per cent thought once a week that they were possibly under threat. That threat tended to be mild (for example, thin king

'Someone's deliberately trying to irritate me') rather than severe ('Someone has it in for me').

We can see that about a third of the population are regularly bothered by suspicious or paranoid thoughts. (You can find the full details of this survey in the table in section entitled "Survey Results")

These statistics may seem surprising. I know I've sometimes felt that way, you may be thinking, but I had no idea that so many other people have had the same feelings. One explanation for this surprise may be that most people find it very difficult to talk about these sorts of worries with those closest to them. No one, after all, wants to be seen as anxious or fearful. No one wants to be labelled as 'paranoid'. Even if we do summon the courage to voice our fears, we often dismiss them in the same breath: 'I'm probably just being paranoid, but...'

In some ways it's hardly surprising that so many of us share these sorts of concerns. Society frequently actually encourages us to be suspicious and fearful. Our news papers are filled with stories of violent crime. Conspiracy theories abound. Crime has apparently reached such high levels that CCTV cameras are required in every town centre. Governments warn us to be on the look out for terrorist threats and seek to combat this and other dangers by monitoring our emails and use of the Internet.

We are taught from an early age that the world is a dangerous place. Of course, in certain contexts it is. Being wary of others is sometimes the most sensible strategy.

However, this book doesn't focus on justified anxieties about others, but rather on *unfounded fears* – fears for which there is no convincing evidence.

Unfounded worries about others don't help us stay safe but instead can bring all manner of distress. Thankfully these kinds of feelings are not inevitable. In the following pages you will learn how to understand your unfounded fears. We will show you how to develop strategies to cope with such fears – and, in so doing, how to put an end to any distressing emotions you may be feeling and move on with your life.

Throughout the book we draw on the methods and insights of cognitive therapy. This approach was first developed as a therapy for depression but has since been used highly successfully to help people deal with a wide range of problems. Cognitive therapy has been explained by the psychologist Gillian Butler as, 'based on the recognition that thoughts and feelings are closely related. If you *think* something is going to go wrong, you will *feel* anxious; if you *think* everything will go fine, you *feel* more confident.' If we can understand and change the way we think and the beliefs we hold, we are able to change the way we feel and the way we behave.

In this opening chapter we'll talk in more detail about what suspicious thoughts are and what they are not. We will spend a little time distinguishing between helpful and unhelpful suspicions. And we'll help you judge which category your concerns fall into.

Assessing your suspicious thoughts

If you would like to assess your own suspicious feelings and anxieties, have a look at the questionnaire below. Remember that suspicious thoughts and fears about others are very common. Having them isn't necessarily a sign that you have a 'problem': suspicious thoughts can be a reasonable and sensible response to everyday life. However, if you have any of the thoughts listed below about once a week or more, or if there have been periods in your life when you have had them, then this book is likely to be of particular interest to you.

I get the feeling that...	Rarely	Once a month	Once a week	Several times a week	Once a day
I need to be on my guard against others.					
Negative comments about me might be being put around.					

I get the feeling that...	Rarely	Once a month	Once a week	Several times a week	Once a day
People deliberately try to irritate me.					
I might be being observed or followed.					
People are trying to make me upset.					
People communicate about me in subtle ways.					
Strangers and friends look at me critically.					
People might be hostile towards me.					
Bad things are being said about me behind my back.					
Someone I know has bad intentions towards me.					
I suspect that someone has it in for me.					
People would harm me if given an opportunity.					

I get the feeling that...	Rarely	Once a month	Once a week	Several times a week	Once a day
Someone I don't know has bad intentions towards me.					
There is a possibility of a conspiracy against me.					
People are laughing at me.					
I am under threat from others.					
I can detect coded messages about me in the press/TV/radio.					
My actions and thoughts might be controlled by others.					

Survey Results

I get the feeling that...	Rarely	Once a month	Once a week	Several times a week	Once a day
I need to be on my guard against others.	31%	17%	21%	21%	10%
Negative comments about me might be being put around.	35%	24%	21%	14%	7%
People de- liberately try to irri- tate me.	57%	17%	15%	8%	4%
I might be being ob- served or followed.	67%	14%	8%	7%	4%
People are trying to make me upset.	72%	16%	7%	4%	1%
People communi- cate about me in sub- tle ways.	52%	22%	14%	9%	3%

I get the feeling that...	Rarely	Once a month	Once a week	Several times a week	Once a day
Strangers and friends look at me critically.	29%	23%	21%	18%	9%
People might be hostile towards me.	45%	27%	16%	9%	4%
Bad things are being said about me behind my back.	45%	25%	15%	11%	4%
Someone I know has bad intentions towards me.	71%	16%	6%	4%	2%
I suspect that some one has it in for me.	83%	9%	4%	2%	2%
People would harm me if given an opportunity.	83%	9%	4%	2%	2%
Someone I don't know has bad intentions towards me.	82%	10%	3%	3%	2%

I get the feeling that...	Rarely	Once a month	Once a week	Several times a week	Once a day
There is a possibility of a conspiracy against me.	90%	5%	2%	1%	2%
People are laughing at me.	41%	26%	19%	9%	6%
I am under threat from others.	76%	13%	5%	3%	2%
I can detect coded messages about me in the press/TV/radio.	96%	2%	1%	1%	1%
My actions and thoughts might be controlled by others.	81%	10%	3%	3%	2%

What are suspicious thoughts?

We could have called this section, 'What are fears about others?' We could also have titled it, 'What are paranoid feelings?' or 'What are persecutory beliefs?'

The feelings we discuss in this book go by a variety of names. As you may already have noticed we make use of them all in this book. Some of these names may be familiar to you, others less so. You may also feel that some are preferable to others (the term 'paranoia', for example, has negative connotations for many people). If you do find any of the terms we use unhelpful, we apologize and hope that you will understand that we want to reflect all of the many names that people use when they describe these sorts of experience.

So what are suspicious or paranoid thoughts? We use the term to mean:

- The fear of something bad happening
- The belief that others may intend to cause such an event.

Here are some examples of suspicious thoughts:

Ian, a 21-year-old engineering student: *Sometimes I may walk down the street and see a group of people standing around talking. If they start laughing as I walk past, I worry that they're actually laughing at me.* **Keith, a 53-year-old postal worker:** *I feel that people – particularly colleagues at work – hate me and are constantly trying to put me down.*

Emily, a 34-year-old solicitor: *I was at a party recently and the thought crossed my mind* *that some people there were saying negative things about me behind my back.*

Cameron, a 26-year-old photographer: *My ex-girlfriend's family are persecuting me; they make me hear voices and they want me to disappear.*

These four experiences are very different to each other in several ways: for instance, the people suspected of harmful intentions; the nature of that harm; and the frequency of the suspicious thoughts.

The experience of persecutory beliefs also varies greatly in severity. Ian's experience is probably something all of us have been through at one time or another; Cameron's feelings are characteristic of someone whose difficulties with these sorts of worries have led him to seek clinical assistance and are less common. (As in Cameron's case, the most severe experiences of persecutory beliefs may be accompanied by what we call *auditory hallucinations* – the experience of 'hearing voices' – which will be discussed in more detail in Chapter 2.)

Though most of us will have these worries at some point in our lives they affect us in different ways. The level of distress will vary as will the certainty with which we hold the belief and the extent to which it preoccupies us. Such worries also vary in plausibility. For example the worry that people are talking behind your back is, in most cases, probably more plausible (though not necessarily more justified) than the worry that Mossad are planning to kidnap you.

Our fears can increase in severity for the following reasons: the greater our belief in them; the extent of our preoccupation with them; the degree of our distress; and the more they seem implausible to others. For the great majority of us our worries about others will be relatively non-severe.

As you can see from the examples above our worries about others take all sorts of forms, arise in all sorts of situations and cause varying degrees of distress. But research by psychologists has shown that our fears about harm can be analyzed in terms of four elements of harm. These four elements are:

- Perpetrators of the harm or threat;
- Type of harm or threat;
- Timing of the harm or threat;
- Motivation or reason for the harm or threat.

The following sections use the examples below to provide a little more detail about each of these elements. As you read the sections you may find it helpful to consider your own anxieties in these terms.

Doreen is a 58-year-old shop worker from London: *At work, if I am restocking the shelves and other staff members are* *nearby, I sometimes think they are joking and talking about me, but I know they aren't really.*

Chris, a 26-year-old teacher: *Standing at a bus stop at night when I was back in Liverpool, a group of drunken youths were walking towards me, and I was worried they may be intent on causing trouble or they may try to hurt me.*

Liz, a 24-year-old musician from Bristol: *I once thought a housemate was trying to steal my possessions as I often caught her standing in the corridor near my room and nowhere near her own room. I got really wound up about this and ended up locking some of my valuables in the garden shed. After this I began to have other thoughts – like she was trying to poison me because she was always asking me to eat food that she had made and giving me new foreign alcohol to try.*

Alex, a 42-year-old lorry driver and former soldier from Scotland: *For a while I used to believe that MI5, Mossad and the police were trying to kidnap and torture me.*

Melissa, a 39-year-old mother of three: *I feel that a neighbour is intent upon entering my house and stealing my property.*

Greg, a 19-year-old student: *I could be with a friend and someone rings them on their* *mobile. If they tell the caller they're with me and if the caller then says something I can't hear and the friend I'm with laughs, I always think that the person on the other end of the phone said something horrible about me.*

Richard, a 34-year-old journalist: *I am fearful that my family is trying to physically harm me.*

The perpetrators

As the examples above demonstrate we can suspect absolutely anyone of wanting to do us harm. For Doreen the perpetrators were her colleagues at work. Liz suspected her housemate. Richard worried about the intentions of his family, while for Alex the perpetrators were members of the police force and other governmental organizations. Sometimes we don't know the identity of the people we fear: all we have is a sense of threat. But, even if don't know who it may be, all persecutory beliefs have as a central element the notion of a perpetrator.

The type of threat or harm

Harm doesn't simply mean physical injury. The exact form of the harm a person may fear varies enormously. Here are some common types:

• The feeling that you are being **watched** or being **talked about.** Doreen's and Greg's anxieties are of this type.

• The worry that people are using **hints and double meanings** to threaten you without anyone else noticing. For example Sarah, a 31-year-old marketing executive described how, at a reunion of old friends, someone had made repeated references to a trip to France they'd all been on as teenagers. She worried that this was actually a coded reference to an embarrassing event that had occurred to her on the trip and about which she had told no one. She saw the comments as an implicit threat to reveal her secret.

• The fear of being **physically harmed** – such as being attacked, poisoned or even killed. For example Chris worried about being attacked by youths while out at night; Richard feared that his family wanted to physically harm him.

• **Social harm** – you may, for example, worry about looking bad in the eyes of others; you may suspect that rumours are being spread about you; or you may feel that you are being excluded or ridiculed. Greg's experience is a good example of this.

• You may feel that others are trying to annoy or upset you. Alan, a 40-year-old salesman who came to us for treatment, complained that other people were constantly trying to irritate him by such small means as coughing or dragging their feet when they walked. We call this **psychological harm.**

- The fear of being **financially harmed,** or of **damage to your possessions.** Liz, for example, believed that her housemate was trying to steal her property.

- You may worry that people want to **get rid of you,** for example, by trying to get you dismissed from your job. Alice, a 38-year-old college lecturer, told us that she believed colleagues were trying to undermine her by spreading malicious rumours in order to have her removed from her post.

- People with severe persecutory thoughts may feel that their actions or thoughts are being **interfered with** by others. Brian, a 58-year-old electrician, believed his brain was being tampered with by doctors and ghosts.

Timing of the threat

When do we believe the harm will happen? By now, you probably won't be surprised to learn that there's no single answer to this question. We may think the harm has already happened or is going on right now: Doreen's anxieties, for instance, arose at the moment when her workmates were gathered nearby. The harm may seem imminent (Chris worried that he was about to be attacked) or likely to occur in the near future (remember Melissa's anxieties about her neighbour). On the other hand, the timescales may be much greater, with the harm seemingly months or even years away. It's not uncommon for a combination of timings to be involved: we may believe that harm has occurred, is continuing to occur and will occur again in the future.

The reason or motivation for the harm

Why do we think we are a target for harm? What do we feel we've done to deserve this ill will on the part of others? Some times people have a feeling that they're simply *victims* – that they've done nothing to deserve the threat or persecution they perceive. Take, for example, the case of Hugh, a 61-year-old retired civil servant. He commented: *Seeing a group of youths makes me feel awkward – especially because you know they are more than likely to try to impress their peers. As a result you realize you may be a victim of their youth and peer pressure.*

In other cases people may suspect that they're at risk because of *who they are.* If we think of ourselves as popular and successful we may feel that we're being threatened because others are jealous of our achievements. If we have a negative view of ourselves – for instance, if we feel uncomfortable in social situations – we may feel that others notice this and pick on us.

Lastly, people may believe that the threat is provoked by *something they've done.* They may feel that they're being rightly punished for a serious mistake or misdemeanour, or even something relatively minor: Alex, a 21-year-old student from Bristol, explained his worries in these terms: *Because I won't take part in some activities that everyone is doing and I decide to stand out and not give in to peer pressure, I think that they talk behind my back.*

In the last few pages we've seen just how varied our fears about others are. And yet they share four common elements – what we might describe as four structuring principles. No matter how diverse the content of our fears may be, the elements or principles remain remarkably constant.

We're almost there in our attempt to pin down what we mean by suspicious thoughts. But we need to take one last step. Before we can be absolutely clear about what suspicious thoughts are, we need to examine *what they're not.*

What suspicious thoughts are not

Suspicious thoughts can resemble two other types of psychological experience: *social anxiety and shyness* and *post-traumatic stress disorder.*

Social anxiety and shyness involve a fear of social situations and there can be hardly anyone who hasn't experienced this at some point in their life. We worry that the people around us will think negatively of us – that they'll think we're boring, stupid or out of place. If they feel this way about us, we reason, they'll naturally dislike and avoid us.

You may have noticed that social anxiety and shyness resemble persecutory anxiety, particularly if that persecutory anxiety focuses on fears of social harm. Persecutory thoughts often revolve around the anxiety caused by social situations – as we've seen, social situations are perhaps the most common con text for such worries. With persecutory thoughts, just as with social anxiety and shyness, we worry about being embarrassed, humiliated or rejected by others.

However, there is one very important difference between them: social anxiety and shyness don't involve us feeling that others *deliberately intend* to make us feel foolish or rejected. Central to the experience of persecutory ideas, on the other hand, is the belief that other people *want to harm us.*

If you would like more information on social anxiety and shyness and how it can be treated with cognitive behavioral therapy, Gillian Butler's *Overcoming Social Anxiety and Shyness* provides an excellent guide.

Post-traumatic stress disorder (PTSD) is a term used to describe a range of experiences caused by a traumatic event. Any number of events may trigger PTSD – from mugging or rape to a road accident or military battle. The sufferer may find themselves having persistent and intrusive thoughts about the event long after it has occurred. They may undergo flashbacks when it seems as if the event is happening again.

Such experiences tend to be highly distressing, so much so that the sufferer avoids any situation associated with the traumatic event. For example Christopher, a barrister, was the victim of a violent mugging one evening on a street near his London home. Over time his fears about being attacked again led him to avoid leaving the house, especially after dark.

As with social anxiety and shyness, PTSD seems to overlap with persecutory thoughts. With both, sufferers may fear other people and believe that they are going to hurt them. PTSD, however, is characterized by the strong *link to a traumatic event.*

Post-traumatic stress disorder can be also be helped by cognitive therapy and Claudia Herbert and Ann Wetmore's book, *Overcoming Traumatic Stress,* is a very useful self-help guide.

Suspicious thoughts can be good for you!

But aren't we *right* to be suspicious of others? The world is, after all, sometimes a dangerous and hostile place. From an early age we are taught to be vigilant. As we grow older this teaching is reinforced by, for example, the media, politicians or, as often as not, simply by those around us. The list of those who want to harm us in some way seems to increase by the day: pickpockets, muggers, burglars, child abductors, drug dealers and terrorists. We learn at an early age not to accept lifts from strangers. As we get older we understand that we should keep hold of our belongings when in a public place. We choose our route carefully when walking home at night. At ATM machines we develop a clever routine of entering our PIN codes and withdrawing our money as quickly and as surreptitiously as possible. Such behavior is completely sensible.

Is it really so odd to worry about being secretly monitored by others? Aren't our town centres full of CCTV cameras? Don't many of the world's governments have powers to intercept our phone calls, letters and email? And we have to be realistic: not everyone can be trusted, sometimes not even our family and friends.

Given all this, being wary about the intentions of others seems highly prudent. And it often is. On the other hand, suspicious thoughts can also be a negative influence in our lives as we'll consider in the following section.

When suspicious thoughts are unhelpful

Think back to the comments made earlier by Keith and Emily. Keith felt that he was hated by the people around him and particularly by his colleagues at work. He thought they were constantly trying to put him down. Emily told of how she'd felt that the other people at the party she was attending were saying negative things about her behind her back.

Both Keith and Emily may have been absolutely right. But there are other possibilities. Their fears may have been exaggerated. For instance, Keith may not have been the most popular person in his office, but no one hated him and no one was trying to harm him in any way. Or their anxieties may be unjustified – Emily saw people talking to one another, as they always do at parties, but there was no evidence to suggest they were talking about her. This is when suspicious thoughts become unhelpful: when they are *exaggerated or unrealistic.* When suspicious thoughts are unfounded they no longer help us protect ourselves. Instead we tend to spend a lot of time worrying about our particular fears and anxieties at the expense of other more positive elements in our life. This preoccupation is often accompanied by distress. For example, Emily's experience at the party caused her to think twice about attending such social gatherings in the future, but avoiding these situations didn't help. Instead the lack of social contact made her feel lonely and unhappy.

Keith began to hate going to work and felt anger toward the colleagues he thought were out to get him. Indeed, he began to withdraw from social situations as a whole. But staying at home didn't make his anger disappear. It also brought about a sense of isolation and depression.

Keith's is a relatively severe experience. For many of us the dis tress caused by our unfounded worries about others isn't as pronounced. But it is real and it is damaging. The good news, how ever, is that is not inevitable. As the following chapters will demonstrate, you can do something about it.

How can you tell whether your suspicious thoughts are justified?

We've seen that worries about others are very common and are often sensible. We've also learned that unjustified worries can have a negative impact on your life and emotions. So how can we tell whether our worries are justified or not?

Well, it's not always easy, as you may have discovered. Emily may have suspected others at the party of talking about her behind her back, but how could she prove or disprove this? Keith may have found himself assigned to what he considered to be less interesting work at the post office. But how would he ever know for sure whether this happened because he was disliked by his colleagues or simply because the department needed to reorganize?

The obvious answer in both Keith's and Emily's cases may seem to be to *talk to the people concerned,* This is often very difficult. Even raising worries with friends and family can be a big challenge. It can feel like a confession of weakness – an embarrassing sign that you can't cope. Sometimes, though, that embarrassment is itself a sign that you suspect your fears might be exaggerated. Opening up to others is hard, but if you don't do it you never get another perspective on your worries; you never get the chance to discuss your fears with another person.

If you're struggling to decide whether your suspicious thoughts are justified, ask yourself the following questions:

Eleven key questions

1 Would other people think my suspicions are realistic?
2 What would my best friend say?
3 Have I talked to others about my worries?
4 Is it possible that I have exaggerated the threat?
5 Is there any indisputable evidence for my suspicions?
6 Are my worries based on ambiguous events?
7 Are my worries based on my feelings rather than indisput able evidence?
8 Is it very likely that I would be singled out above anyone else?
9 Is there any evidence that runs contrary to my suspicions?
10 Is it possible that I'm being at all over-sensitive?
11 Do my suspicions persist despite reassurance from others that they are unfounded?

There are no hard and fast rules for deciding for certain whether a worry is realistic. But by asking yourself these questions you can determine the *probability* of the suspicion being justified.

The probability that your fears are *unrealistic* increases the more you feel that:

• No one else fully shares your suspicions;
• There is no indisputable evidence to support your worries;
• There is evidence against your suspicions;
• It is unlikely that you would be singled out;
• Your fears persist despite reassurance from others;
• Your fears are based on feelings and ambiguous events.

Assessing whether or not your fears are realistic is the first step toward achieving the balance we're all aiming for: *being suspicious only when appropriate.*

CHAPTER SUMMARY

• By **suspicious thoughts** we mean the worry that other people intend to cause us harm.
• Such thoughts are extremely common, though they're rarely talked about.
• Suspicious thoughts vary enormously in severity and in content, but it can be helpful to analyze them in terms of their common elements: the

perpetrator of the harm; the nature of the harm; the timing of the harm; and the motivation for the harm.

- Suspicious thoughts can resemble social anxiety and posttraumatic stress disorder, though in fact they are different in certain key aspects.

- In certain circumstances suspicious thoughts can be helpful.

- Unhelpful suspicious thoughts are those that are exaggerated or unrealistic.

- It is often hard to decide whether your suspicions are justified, but asking yourself certain key questions can help.

2

When do we experience paranoid and suspicious thoughts?

'I am not so unreasonable, sir, as to think you at all responsible for my mistakes and wrong conclusions; but I always supposed it was Miss Havisham.'

'As you say, Pip,' returned Mr Jaggers, turning his eyes upon me coolly, and taking a bite at his forefinger, 'I am not at all responsible for that.'

'And yet it looked so like it, sir,' I pleaded with a downcast heart.

'Not a particle of evidence, Pip,' said Mr Jaggers, shaking his head and gathering up his skirts. 'Take nothing on its looks; take every thing on evidence. There's no better rule.'

Charles Dickens, *Great Expectations*

Introduction

One of English literature's best-loved novels is Charles Dickens's *Great Expectations*. It follows the fortunes from childhood to young adulthood of Philip

Pirrip (known to all as 'Pip'), a village boy brought up by his bad-tempered sister and her much more likeable blacksmith husband. As the novel reaches its conclusion we come to see, just as Pip eventually sees for himself, that Pip has misunderstood almost all of the major events – and people – of his life.

For example, when an unknown person makes Pip suddenly rich he assumes that his benefactor is the deranged but apparently wealthy Miss Havisham. He's wrong. Miss Havisham is no one's benefactor; she lives in a mansion certainly, but she has no money. When Miss Havisham brings together Pip and her beautiful protégée Estella, Pip falls deeply in love. He does not see that Estella has been so corrupted by Miss Havisham that she can bring him (and herself) only misery.

The list of misunderstandings is a long one! Pip believes not only that the middle-class world he's moving into is superior to the modest village life he's leaving behind, but that the people in that middle-class world are superior too. He is mistaken on both counts, an error which leads him to abandon the one per son in the world who truly loves him, his blacksmith stepfather Joe Gargery. And when Pip encounters the escaped convict Magwitch he feels fear, repulsion and shame. He has no idea that Magwitch is in fact his mysterious benefactor.

Pip is a master of misinterpretation. Again and again he makes the wrong judgment or draws the wrong conclusion. But we shouldn't be too hard on him. For us all understanding the true meaning of the events and emotions we experience can sometimes be bewilderingly difficult. As *Great Expectations* demonstrates life can be extraordinarily ambiguous; it's not surprising that we occasionally misinterpret things. And our preconceptions, preferences and, let's be honest, our prejudices don't always help us deal with that ambiguity.

You may be wondering what all this has to do with the subject of this chapter: when do we experience suspicious thoughts? The next few pages look at the typical situations in which suspicious thoughts commonly occur. We will see that they are often sparked into life by things around us. We'll see, too, that suspicious thoughts are also frequently related to the way you are feeling inside. But whether the trigger for your fears seems to come from outside (what might be called the external world) or inside (your internal state), those fears reflect your interpretation of what is happening. In trying to make sense of our experiences we make judgments and develop explanations – just like Pip.

Persecutory thoughts don't just occur out of the blue. *They are our attempts to make sense of our experiences.* They are our explanations of the world around us or the way we feel inside. As you read this chapter think about the situations in which you experience suspicious thoughts. Often there are one or two specific details that trigger your suspicions. As preparation for the suggestions we make later in the book for dealing with your fears, try to identify exactly what it is in these situations that you find troubling. Ask yourself these questions: *What sorts of situations trigger my fears? What is it about these situations that seems threatening?*

When do we experience suspicious thoughts?

There are two main types of trigger for suspicious thoughts:

- The situations, events and experiences we encounter in the world;
- The way we feel inside.

These are called *external* and *internal* triggers. Some people's fears are triggered by just one specific experience; for other people their fears may be provoked by a range of situations. Let's start by looking at some common external triggers.

External triggers

Suspicious thoughts often arise when:

- We're in social situations;
- We're in situations from which it is difficult to escape;

- We feel exposed;
- We think we might be blamed, accused, mocked or criticized;
- Unusual events occur;
- We're alone.

Let's explore each of these in more detail.

Social situations

I was at a party recently and the thought crossed my mind that some people there were saying negative things about me behind my back ... I could see a group of people I knew from work chatting together on the other side of the room. I saw them look in my direction a couple of times and then immediately look away. I thought they were maybe feeling guilty or embarrassed about discussing me and that's why they looked away. Later I heard them laughing and wondered whether they were laughing at me.

These comments from Emily, the solicitor we met in Chapter 1, are a good illustration of the ways in which social situations (such as parties or meetings) can trigger suspicions about others. For many people social situations can be stressful events. We may feel a pressure to fit in with the other people there. It can seem as though we're forced to perform. We have to try to be entertaining, amusing, articulate – even just plain polite – when really we'd prefer to be almost anywhere else in the world doing just about anything else!

In situations that provoke these kinds of anxieties it's not surprising that people may interpret what's going on around them negatively. Like Emily, we worry that the laughter we hear is at our expense. If we spot people looking at us while chat ting to someone else, we wonder, just like Emily, whether they're talking about us. We overhear snatches of conversation and can't help feeling that they might relate to us, that rumours are being spread about us. If people don't come up to talk to us, we may assume it's because no one likes us. Even if we are part of a group chatting, other worries can arise. Emily described her experience this way:

Sometimes at parties I'd find myself feeling very distant from the group of people I was talk-ing to. It seemed like I had nothing to contribute to the conversation. Even when I did have some-thing I wan ted to say, the people I was with didn't seem to want to hear it. Then I'd worry that, because I couldn't join in with the conversa-tion, the others would think I was stupid. I'd think, 'I don't belong here, I don't fit in.' Some-times (and this seems very odd), I'd almost feel as if I weren't there at all – like I'd somehow vanished.

These kinds of anxieties naturally make it very difficult for us to enjoy the occasion. And amidst all the stress, amidst all the troubling little details of the evening – the comment overheard, the glance from a colleague – is the sense that it's so hard to be sure whether what we've noticed is really going on or not. This feeling of uncertainty is common to all the situations you will read about in this chapter. We rarely know for sure whether someone means us harm. It's worth keeping this crucial point in mind as you read the following sections, and it's also worth thinking about its relevance to your own experiences.

Situations from which it is difficult to escape

I sometimes find bus journeys and trips on trains difficult. If someone looks at me it can feel like they're weighing me up. I don't know why. And when they look away, back down to their book or paper or whatever, it's as though they can't bear to look at me any more. If the seat next to me is free and someone gets on and doesn't take the seat it makes me feel as though there's something wrong with me. I look at the person they're sitting next to and wonder why they chose that person and not me. Other times someone might sit down next to me and it feels as if they've done it deliberately to crowd my space – they're leaning into me or rustling their paper really loudly or something. Once I was on the train and the guy next to me was coughing every five seconds. It felt like he was doing it on purpose to annoy me even though I knew he wasn't.

These comments from Melissa, a 23-year-old student from London, capture perfectly the sort of persecutory thoughts that can be triggered when we're stuck somewhere for a while. Bus and train journeys are typical examples of this and you might have had similar experiences in lifts or on car journeys with friends or family.

For Todd, a 30-year-old journalist, crowded cinemas could provoke these kinds of worries:

I'd feel trapped. I hated the embarrassment of having to ask so many people to move in order to escape. I could feel myself becoming more and more uptight. Sometimes I got really panicky. The sound of the film suddenly seemed deafening. I couldn't bear to look at the screen because the colours were so intense. I felt like speaking to the man ager – they were screening the film in some weird way for some weird reason. What were they trying to do to us? If someone opened a bag of sweets three rows away it sounded like an explosion.

If someone whispered to their companion, I'd hear it as loud as if they were yelling through a megaphone. And I'd think they were doing it deliberately to annoy me.

SITUATIONS IN WHICH WE FEEL EXPOSED

Being out and about can sometimes make us feel very vulnerable. Alone, and out of reach of the safety of home, our perception of the world and the people around us changes. Suddenly it can seem as if we are surrounded by potential danger. In Chapter 1 Ian, a 21-year-old engineering student told us:

Some times I may walk down the street and see a group of people standing around talking. If they start laughing as I walk past I worry that they're actually laughing at me. I tend to deal with this by trying to hurry past them. I make sure I don't look at them in case I draw more attention to myself. If someone bumps into me I wonder whether they did it deliberately.

It's likely that we've all felt like this from time to time, particularly when walking home alone at night. Sharon is a 41-year-old mother of three. Her comments provide another insight into the worries that feeling exposed can provoke:

If I'm in town, in a shop or something, and someone looks at me, I might wonder what they're up to. There are times when, for some reason, I find all sorts of things suspicious: someone sitting on a bench, someone talking on a mobile phone, even someone wearing sunglasses when it isn't very sunny. If they look in my direction I think there must be a reason and that it may involve me – maybe they're planning something. In the park the other day some kids were messing around and yelling really loudly.

I thought, they're doing it on purpose to annoy me. Actually, I don't think they'd even noticed I was there.

Just like the other examples of situations in which people can feel suspicious, when we feel exposed relatively insignificant details in the world around us – for example, the fact that someone is sitting on a bench – can suddenly seem important signs that someone means us harm.

SITUATIONS IN WHICH WE MIGHT BE BLAMED, ACCUSED, MOCKED OR CRITICIZED

In Chapter 1 we mentioned Sarah, a 31-year-old marketing executive. Sarah was worried that, at a reunion of old friends, people were dropping unkind hints about an embarrassing event that had happened to her on a school trip to France:

I'd gone into a supermarket to buy some chocolate as a present for my grandmother. I ended up with a trolley full of stuff! But while I was shopping I decided – why, I've no idea – to see if I could sneak something past the cashier. I'd never stolen anything before that and I've never stolen anything since. Anyway, I put my bag in the trolley and hid a packet of sweets underneath it. I thought I'd be able to push the trolley past the cashier without her noticing the sweets. But I was just about to pay when the woman behind me noticed the sweets. I don't know whether she or the cashier knew what I was up to. They were very pleasant and acted as if I must have just forgotten the sweets. But I felt awful – I still feel awful about it – and I couldn't wait to get out of there. I never told anyone about what had happened.

Doing something wrong, or just feeling as though we have, is frequently a trigger for persecutory thoughts. The actual deed may well be a very minor one – a malicious thought, a mistake at work or (as in Sarah's case) a youthful indiscretion. But we worry that other people know about it and dislike and even punish us for it. We may feel that, though we've told no one about our mistake, the sense of guilt and shame is plain to see on our face. It can seem, as it did to Sarah, that the consequences of our actions will last for years.

But sometimes it's not the fact that we've done something wrong that provokes persecutory thoughts – it's simply the feeling that we're in a situation in which *we might be accused of doing wrong.* The writer Alan Bennett provides a telling example of this in his diary where he describes going blackberry picking:

I blackberry up the lane that leads to Wharfe ... My nightmare when blackberrying (or when I stop the car for a pee) is that I shall find the body of a child, that I will report it and be suspected of the crime. So I find myself running through in my mind the evidences of my legitimate occupation – where I started picking, who saw me park, and so on.

What emerges so clearly from this extract is the way in which the situation – the deserted country lane – evokes such a powerful sense of vulnerability in Alan Bennett. Of course it's not just any type of vulnerability: it's specifically vulnerability to accusation, to the mistaken thoughts and actions of others. If something does happen, who will there be to act as a witness to his innocence?

If the mere possibility of accusation can provoke persecutory fears, it's hardly surprising that such fears can also be sparked when *we have actually been criticized or mocked.* In the previous chapter we heard about Alice, a lecturer who believed that there was a plot to remove her from her job. This belief had its roots in an angry but apparently trivial exchange Alice had had several months before with a colleague in a meeting. The colleague had seemed to criticize the way Alice taught a particular course. This incident left Alice feeling that the colleague was pursuing a vendetta against her. Moreover, she worried that others at the meeting who'd witnessed the argument would share the colleague's criticism of her. Every time she saw the colleague, and eventually every time she met someone who'd also been at the meeting, her anxiety grew.

WHEN UNUSUAL EVENTS OCCUR

Earlier in this chapter Sharon told us:

There are times, when for some reason, I find all sorts of things suspicious: someone sitting on a bench, someone talking on a mobile phone, even someone wearing sunglasses when it isn't very sunny.

Wearing sunglasses on a cloudy day might seem to many of us an odd thing to do, but for Sharon it's more than odd: it's a sign of possible threat. Like Sharon, many people who experience suspicious thoughts find them triggered by apparently odd or unusual events. Events that are almost certainly co-incidental can start to seem connected. We might, for example, worry if we spot the same car behind us at several points in a journey or if we see the same person in the street two or three times. For Liz, the musician we heard from in Chapter 1, finding her flatmate on more than one occasion in the hall-way near Liz's bedroom sparked the belief that the flatmate was planning to steal items from her room. She began to feel that things in her room had been disturbed or rearranged, reinforcing her worries about her flatmate. *Unusual events, coincidences and apparent connections* can all make us suspect that there's more going on than meets the eye and that other people mean us harm.

WHEN WE'RE ALONE

For many of us it's only when we are alone and reflecting on the day's events that suspicious thoughts occur. Only then do we remember and begin to consider the little details that so often are sufficient to prompt our anxieties. In the previous chapter we heard about the experiences of Keith, who came to feel that his colleagues at the postal sorting office where he worked were hostile to him. Keith told us:

It became a habit. I'd get home from work, make myself a cup of tea and try to read the paper or have a nap. But then I'd find myself thinking back through the day. And then all kinds of things that hadn't bothered me at the time – a comment someone had made, a look I thought someone had given me – started to worry me.

Keith attempted to deal with his anxieties by avoiding work and social situations as much as possible. But isolation can just leave us with more time on our hands to dwell on our worries, while also depriving us of the opportunity to disprove our fears. If you never spend time with the people you think are hostile to you, you never have the chance to find out whether they are or not.

The preceding few pages have outlined the variety of situations that commonly trigger suspicious thoughts. Varied though the situations are, it's often the same types of information that seem to contribute to our anxieties:

- **Non-verbal signs,** such as people's expressions, hand gestures, or the way someone is dressed;
- **Verbal signs,** for example something that is said to us or snatches of conversation we overhear,

particularly when we think the comment is unpleasant or when we're not sure who or what it refers to;

• **Coincidences and unusual events,** for example seeing the same car behind us several times throughout a journey or hearing things we've said apparently repeated by someone else.

These kinds of information are almost always ambiguous – they could mean any number of things. And yet we place so much weight on our interpretations. This is natural: like Pip in *Great Expectations* we want to make sense of our experiences. But after a while you may find that your interpretations start to change the way you approach certain situations. If you've felt out of place and awkward at social events, the latest invitation only fills you with dread. If you've come to suspect that a colleague doesn't like you, you're apprehensive every time you have to deal with him or her. We begin to *expect* to have a negative experience. *We take our explanations of past events and project them on to the future.* The smallest gesture or most offhand comment is enough to confirm our suspicions. Yet the extent to which these events affect us is often highly dependent on how we feel inside, and it's these *internal triggers* that will be looked at now.

Internal triggers

The common internal triggers for suspicious thoughts include:

- Our **emotions** – for example feelings of anxiety, unhappiness, guilt, shame, anger, disgust and even in some cases elation;
- Feelings of **arousal** – by which we mean a feeling of being especially alert and sensitive;
- Changes in the way we **perceive** the world around us, for example the way things look or sound or smell. We call these sorts of feelings **anomalous experiences;**
- Inebriation through **drugs** or **alcohol.**

The following pages look in more detail at each of these.

OUR EMOTIONS

It probably won't surprise you to learn that we're much less likely to experience suspicious thoughts when we're feeling happy, calm and focused on a task.

In contrast, the most common emotional trigger for feelings of paranoia is **anxiety.** Keith's experiences provide an excellent illustration of this:

It got to the stage where I dreaded going to work. I slept badly the night before. I could feel myself tensing up on the journey in. By the time I reached the building I was in a right state: heart pounding, headache, sweating – the lot. I had to really fight the temptation to just turn around and go home. Eventually I gave in to that temptation and stayed away altogether.

When you're feeling this way it's much more likely that you'll make negative interpretations of the things that happen to you. After all, it's hard to make cool, calm judgments when we're so tense. Keith's anxiety became the perfect platform for his persecutory fears, making him feel so on edge that any ambiguous behavior from colleagues was likely to be seen by him as hostile.

The second major emotional trigger is **low mood.** Low mood is a catch-all term used for the variety of ways in which people can feel down – for instance, feeling miserable, sad or depressed; having reduced energy levels or little interest in life; or feeling bad about ourselves, maybe because of a sense of shame or guilt or the belief that we're alone, worthless, unloved or a failure. As with anxiety low mood seems to make us susceptible to our fears about others. In some cases the effect low mood has on our behavior can prompt the very events that we interpret as suspicious. For example, if you're feeling depressed you may not feel like chatting to friends or colleagues. Other people pick up on this and leave you alone. You may then start to worry that they are excluding you.

Low mood features in the stories of several of the people in this book. In Chapter 1 Greg explained:

I could be with a friend and someone rings them on their mobile. If they tell the caller they're with me and if the caller then says something I can't hear and the friend I'm with laughs, I always think that the per son on the other end of the phone said something horrible about me.

Greg was asked why he thought people were saying horrible things about him:

I don't know ... I guess I don't have a very high opinion of myself and I expect others to feel the same way about me.

Emily told us about her difficulties in social situations:

I'd worry that, because I couldn't join in with the conversation, the others would think I was stupid. I'd think, 'I don't belong here, I don't fit in.' ... That feeling of not belonging, of being different and isolated, is actually something I've experienced at various times of my life. It comes and goes. I've no idea where it comes from.

The hostility Emily and Greg detect in others reflects the way they feel about themselves. Their persecutory thoughts are able to build on, and take advantage of, their low mood. The way we feel about ourselves appears to have a big influence on how we interpret events – and specifically our sense of how others feel about us. It's as if we're trying to make that leap into the wide world around us, to really understand what's going on, but we keep running into the wall of our emotions.

Two other emotions worth mentioning here are **anger** and **elation.** When we're angry the little problems and irritations of life seem to have much more of an effect on us. We feel irritated, wound up, on edge. Our fuse is shorter. When we're in a mood like this suspicious thoughts are more likely to pop into our heads. We may start to feel that the child sitting next to us on the bus is sniffing every thirty seconds just to wind us up even further, or that the man who bumps into us as we get off has done so on purpose.

Elation, a feeling of exceptional happiness, is a less common trigger for persecutory worries, but one that does affect a number of people. With feelings of elation can come a sense that we're different from others, that we're particularly blessed: that we are *special.* We may expect other people to be aware of our specialness and to treat us accordingly. When we don't receive the recognition we feel we deserve, we may conclude that this is a calculated slight on the part of others – we feel that they're deliberately trying to undermine us.

FEELINGS OF AROUSAL

Let's return to Keith's description of his anxiety at the prospect of going to work:

> *I could feel myself tensing up on the journey in. By the time I reached the building I was in a right state: heart pounding, headache, sweating*

– the lot. I had to really fight the temptation to just turn around and go home.

Keith's emotional response to this stressful situation puts him in a state of *arousal,* a state of unusual alertness. We might feel our heart beat faster or have butterflies in our stomach. Our mind is buzzing with thoughts; we feel on edge, perhaps even out of control. Arousal is the body's way of dealing with a potentially dangerous situation. We may not even be conscious of that danger but our body is gearing up for action.

Arousal is associated with a range of emotions, including those we've just been looking at – anxiety, low mood, anger and elation. But it's not just emotions that can cause arousal: drugs and alcohol can do it and we'll discuss these later in this chapter. Arousal can be brought about by having to deal with traumatic or highly stressful situations (for example, a bereavement, or lack of money or problems in our relationships). Lack of sleep is another common trigger. Keith's nightmarish journeys to work were frequently preceded by sleepless nights, for instance, and we're all familiar with the very strange feelings that sleeplessness can cause.

All of these experiences can change the way we feel about ourselves and the world, knocking us out of our usual, comfortable stride and putting us on our guard. And since arousal is a sign that we sense danger, it's perhaps not surprising that these feelings are often the backdrop to suspicious thoughts in which other people are the danger.

ANOMALOUS EXPERIENCES

Anomalous experiences are closely linked to arousal. Arousal is our body on edge, sensing danger and preparing to flee or fight. For most of us, arousal is a departure from the norm – we don't usually feel this way. When we're aroused our bodies, our minds and the world around us can feel very different. Things can app ear brighter or more vivid; sounds can seem louder and more intrusive. In fact, any of our senses can be affected. We might become unusually sensitive to smells; objects might seem odd to the touch.

These altered perceptions of ourselves and the world are called anomalous experiences. As with arousal, there is a lot of evidence to suggest that people are more prone to the range of anomalous experiences when they've lost someone close, or suffered some other traumatic event, or when they've gone without sleep for an extended period. Anomalous experiences are very common and in fact are not always unpleasant. But when people try to account for them, they can be a trigger for suspicious thoughts. Earlier in this chapter we heard about Scott's experience in crowded cinemas:

I could feel myself becoming more and more uptight. Sometimes I got really panicky. The sound of the film suddenly seemed deafening. I couldn't bear to look at the screen because the colours were so intense. I felt like speaking to the manager – they were screening the film in some weird way for some weird reason. What were they trying to do to us? If someone opened a bag of sweets three rows away it sounded like an explosion. If someone whispered to their companion, I'd hear it as loud as if they were yelling through a megaphone. And I'd think they were doing it deliberately to annoy me.

Scott's claustrophobic anxiety escalates until he's experiencing his surroundings in some very unusual ways. And when he tries to make sense of these experiences, he wonders whether they're caused deliberately by other people.

Other common types of anomalous experience include feeling as though:

- Our thoughts aren't our own;
- Apparently insignificant events are actually highly significant;
- The world isn't real;
- We ourselves don't exist.

Psychologists call this last one *depersonalization* and it's something Emily has sometimes felt at parties:

Occasionally (and this seems very odd), I'd almost feel as if I weren't there at all – like I'd somehow vanished. I'd feel this especially if I was on my own, or finding it difficult to join in a con-

versation. I'd be incredibly conscious of all these people laughing and having fun and it seemed like I was just a void in comparison, somehow lightweight and invisible.

As you'll have seen from the examples above, anomalous experiences come in a variety of forms. But perhaps the most 'notorious' is *hallucinations* – when we see or hear things that haven't actually occurred. (These sorts of experience are also often referred to as *illusions* or *hearing voices.*)

Hallucinations are actually very common: studies indicate that around 10–15 per cent of us experience them at some point during our lives. They aren't only associated with periods of anxiety and stress; for example, many people describe hearing voices as they fall asleep at night or first thing in the morning as they wake up. Just like the other internal triggers we've looked at it's the way we try to make sense of hallucinations that can lead to suspicious thoughts. For many of us the 'explanation' is that they are caused by the actions of other people.

INEBRIATION THROUGH DRUGS OR ALCOHOL

Surveys indicate that large numbers of people take 'recreational' drugs such as cannabis, ecstasy and cocaine. For some it's an enjoyable experience; others feel that any negative effects are made up for by the positive feelings the drug gives them.

Clearly drugs don't make everyone who uses them paranoid. However for some people they can make suspicious thoughts more likely to occur. Cannabis (or grass, weed, reefers, skunk, marijuana, ganja, hashish) in particular is commonly associated with feelings of paranoia. A wide range of other drugs can also play a part in triggering suspicious thoughts:

• Stimulants – such as amphetamines (speed), cocaine, khat, ecstasy and even caffeine if we drink enough of it;
• Hallucinogens – for example, LSD (acid) and mescaline;
• Glue and other solvents;
• Alcohol – when drunk regularly in large quantities.

Drugs can lead to persecutory thoughts because they change the way we perceive the world and the way we feel inside. They can cause arousal and anomalous experiences. For example we may feel detached or unreal; or we might find ourselves in a state of heightened sensitivity, even to the extent of feeling out of control. We might feel panicky or things can leap into our onsciousness that seem especially significant or special. Hallucino gens (as their name suggests) can trigger Hallucinations.

The range of effects that drugs can have on us is huge, but what they have in common is this alteration of our normal state. Some people find this pleasurable. For others the changes drugs bring about feed into suspicious thoughts. When we try to understand these changes in the way we feel and perceive the world around us, we may see in them evidence that other people want to harm us. In most cases, these feelings disappear once the drug is out of our system, but for some people the effects can last longer. If you do get suspicious thoughts and are using drugs, you may want to consider whether the drugs are a factor.

***

As you'll probably have noticed, there are many similarities between the various internal triggers for suspicious thoughts:

- We feel **different inside,** which can make us feel vulnerable.
- We feel **aroused,** with heightened sensitivity to the world around us. We may feel things are getting out of control.
- We have **anomalous experiences.** Sounds can seem louder and more intrusive than normal and colours too vivid. We might feel that we, or the world around us, aren't real. And we may experience hallucinations.

When we feel like this, all sorts of things that would normally seem trivial can suddenly take on huge importance. We feel odd inside and we notice odd things in the world around us – it can easily seem as if something is wrong. And when we try to understand what we're experiencing we can begin to suspect that other people are to blame.

Medical and psychiatric conditions

Suspicious thoughts are very common. One recent survey suggested that 70 per cent of people have had such feelings at some point in their lives.

Paranoia, then, is something almost everyone has experienced. You could say it's normal. However, it is also associated with a number of specific medical conditions which we'll dis cuss in the next couple of pages. Having suspicious thoughts doesn't mean that you have any of these conditions and it doesn't mean that you're going to develop them. But if you *do* have one of these medical conditions you're much more likely to also have strong persecutory thoughts.

PSYCHIATRIC DISORDERS

At present in the UK there are somewhere between half a million and a million people who have been diagnosed as suffering from *psychosis.*

The term psychosis actually covers a number of psychiatric conditions (or mental illnesses), including *schizophrenia* and *bipolar disorder.* People with these illnesses can sometimes experience very powerful paranoia. They can have strong beliefs that others don't share (known as *delusions)*. They can hear voices when no one is around, and see and feel things that people around them don't see or feel (*hallucinations*). Often the voices that people hear are very critical. Cameron, the 26-year-old photographer who we heard from in Chapter 1, provides a typical example of this sort of experience:

> *My ex-girlfriend's family are persecuting me. They want me to disappear. They make me hear these voices – the voices are always negative, always horrible, always putting me down.*

It's worth remembering that it's not just people diagnosed with psychosis who experience hallucinations and delusions. Lots of us have these experiences, cope perfectly well and enjoy good mental health. It is when these experiences are so strong that they interfere significantly with our lives that people are said to have mental illness. For those who *are* dealing with psychosis, the ways in which it affects them are very varied. For some it's a one-off experience; for others it's an occasional occurrence; for still others it's continuous.

We should bear in mind too that even among the psychological and medical professions there's a lot of debate about how helpful diagnoses like psychosis or schizophrenia really are. There's a great deal of stigma attached to these conditions: it can be a very negative label for people to deal with. And there's a bigger point: how useful are these terms for psychiatric disorder when there's no real agreement on what mental illness really is? After all, it's hard to draw a clear dividing line between good mental health and mental illness. For many of us our mental health is better at some times than others.

This isn't to say that these diagnoses are never useful. They do help identify people who are likely to be severely affected by paranoia. And some people living with these conditions can find the diagnosis helpful – it puts a name to the experiences they've been undergoing. Also, diagnoses help medical staff decide on appropriate medication (medication is discussed in the Appendix to this book).

However, despite the controversies concerning the nature of mental health and diagnoses such as psychosis and schizophrenia, there's lots of evidence to suggest that the approach we outline in this book based on the ideas of cognitive therapy can be beneficial for everyone experiencing suspicious thoughts, whether you're suffering from mental illness or not. You might remember from Chapter 1 that cognitive therapy is based on the principle that if we can understand and change the way we think, we can change the way we feel. A recent British Psychological Society report states:

The most common form of psychological therapy for psychotic experiences is Cognitive Behavior Therapy – CBT. This is a tried and tested intervention that examines patterns of thinking associated with a range of emotional and behavioral problems. There is convincing evidence that psychological interventions are effective for many people in reducing psychotic experiences and the distress and disability they cause.

You can find details of this report and a list of helpful books and Web sites in Further Reading. As we've mentioned though, cognitive therapy – and specifically the strategies for dealing with suspicious thoughts we set out in this book – can help a wide range of people. The key thing is the *distress* that our suspicious thoughts cause. If the distress is mild, you may need to do little more than read this book. If it's more pronounced you may want to be more active in using the ideas we go on to talk about. If the distress is really troubling for you it might be advisable to seek professional assistance to help you work through the ideas we set out. Some pointers to useful organizations and resources are provided in the section called Useful Organizations.

OTHER MEDICAL CONDITIONS

In addition to psychiatric disorders there are a number of other medical conditions that can trigger suspicious thoughts. If you or a relative have any of these conditions you may find it helpful to be aware of the connection – you might, for example, want to discuss the issue with your doctor.

- **Hearing loss:** Loss of hearing is common as we grow older and it can sometimes be a factor in the development of suspicious thoughts. After all, if we can't hear what's being said, we might well worry that people are talking behind our backs.

• **Dementia:** Suspicious thoughts often occur in older people who are developing dementia (for example, Alzheimer's dis ease). Dementia makes people confused and disorientated and makes it much harder for them to make sense of events. The suspicious thoughts often focus on the worry that the sufferer's property is going to be, or has been, stolen.

• **Alcohol and drug dependency:** Earlier in this chapter we discussed the way suspicious thoughts can be triggered by drugs or alcohol. The link is even greater for people who have alcohol and drug dependency problems (often called 'addictions').

• **Epilepsy:** For a small number of people suffering from epilepsy, the illness seems to trigger suspicious thoughts. This is particularly the case for people with temporal lobe epilepsy.

CHAPTER SUMMARY

• There are two main types of trigger for suspicious thoughts – the situations, events and experiences we encounter in the world and the way we feel inside. These are called **external** and **internal** triggers.

- Common external triggers are: social situations; situations from which it's difficult to escape; unusual events; solitude; when we feel exposed; and situations in which we think we might be blamed, accused, mocked or criticized.
- Common internal triggers are: our emotions; feelings of arousal; anomalous experiences; and when we've taken drugs or drunk excessive alcohol.
- For both internal and external triggers suspicious thoughts are brought about by our attempts to **make sense of ambiguous events or feelings:** we think that **other people** may be to blame.
- Suspicious thoughts are also associated with a number of medical and psychiatric conditions, though having these sorts of thoughts doesn't necessarily mean you either have one of these conditions or are about to develop it.

3

Common reactions to paranoid and suspicious thoughts

Introduction

At the beginning of this book we defined what suspicious thoughts are, and we also discovered that they are amazingly widespread. Almost everyone at some stage of their lives experience these sorts of worries. In Chapter 2 we described the common triggers for suspicious thoughts – the events or feelings that seem to spark these experiences. This chapter looks at the various ways in which people *react* to suspicious thoughts. We begin by identifying the most common reactions. We then present the results of a survey of over a thousand people. The survey shows which of these common reactions people feel are the most helpful and which ones are the least helpful. The chapter ends with a questionnaire to help you analyze your own reactions to suspicious thoughts.

All of the reactions looked at in this chapter are understandable responses to what can be quite disturbing experiences. However, as you will see, some of them are likely to make us feel better and some will probably make the problem worse. *How we react has a big impact on how well we cope with suspicious thoughts.* If you're not coping as well as you'd like with suspicious thoughts, you may find that changing the way you res pond to them can make a real difference. As you read through the following pages think about the way you react to suspicious thoughts and consider the reactions that other people find helpful.

Common reactions

The typical responses to suspicious thoughts are:

- **Ignoring** them;
- Taking a **problem-solving** approach;
- Responding **emotionally;**
- **Avoiding** them;
- Treating them as if they might be **correct;**
- Trying to **understand** them.

In a moment we'll look at each of these reactions in detail. But before we do it's worth mentioning that our reactions to suspicious thoughts may involve a combination of these responses and may vary a lot depending on the situation. Over time too, we may find that the reactions we used to find helpful no longer work so well.

Ignoring suspicious thoughts

Emily is the 34-year-old solicitor whose anxiety in social situations was looked at in the previous two chapters. We asked Emily whether she could remember a time when social events *hadn't* triggered suspicious thoughts. She told us:

Well, sometimes it feels like it's been this way forever. But actually I think it's something that's developed since university. Before that either I didn't have the thoughts or, when I did, they just didn't seem important. For example, I do remember being at parties when I was at college and on the odd occasion wondering whether people were laughing at me, and there was one girl I actually half-suspected might be speaking about me behind my back. But it was as if the thoughts popped into my head and popped right out again. I never spent any time worrying about them.

It's striking that, though Emily has had suspicious thoughts for a long time, *they haven't always been a problem for her.* In fact, their effect on her used to be so insignificant that it didn't seem to matter to her whether she had them or not. Either way, they didn't have any impact. If suspicious thoughts did occur, Emily took no notice: *she ignored them.*

You might be surprised to learn that ignoring suspicious thoughts is actually the most common reaction. It might suddenly occur to us that another person is behaving suspiciously, but we don't let the thought affect us. We carry on with what we're doing and think no more about it. *We let the thought go.* Just like Emily people often do this without making a conscious decision. If we think about the thought at all, it's only to the extent of noticing it as a thought. But we don't see it as true or important: it's just another of the thousands of thoughts we have each day, most of which, like this one, we soon forget.

Remember that this approach doesn't mean not having suspicious thoughts – and it's not a question of trying to avoid them either. Suspicious thoughts occur, but we simply ignore them, generally without even trying. Later in this book we'll find out why many people find it so difficult to deal like this with suspicious thoughts. That said, if we think back hard enough, most of us can remember a time when we managed to ignore a suspicious thought and get on with what we were doing.

The problem-solving approach

Rather than just ignoring suspicious thoughts, some people analyze them calmly and carefully. When we adopt this approach, *suspicious thoughts are a problem to be solved.* We try to discover why they're occurring and whether they're accurate. We look for evidence – and particularly evidence that the thoughts aren't true. We might also ask other people for advice on how to deal with them. We try to put them in context and look at the wider picture, for example by remembering the occasions when people have been kind or supportive.

The emotional response

One of the worst things about the situation was the fact that, once I'd begun to worry that I wasn't wanted at work, it seemed impossible to shake off the thoughts. As they got stronger, and happened more often, I felt overwhelmed by them – it made me really miserable. I'd try to concentrate on other things but found that I couldn't. I was disgusted with myself. I felt like I should have been able to deal with the situation. I was sure other people would have handled it much better than me.

These comments from Keith, the postal worker we've heard from several times already in this book, give an excellent insight into the emotional response to suspicious thoughts. In this reaction we don't ignore our suspicions, neither do we try to analyze them. Instead, we take them to heart: *they upset us.* We may feel hopeless or frustrated. Our worries seem a sign of our weakness. They dominate our lives and there seems to be nothing we can do about it. The situation is often made worse by the sense that we really *ought* to be able to cope with these sorts of thoughts.

Avoiding suspicious thoughts

Although we may feel that our suspicions aren't justified, the distress they cause can prompt us to *avoid the situations that trigger these thoughts.* In Chapter 2 we heard how Ian, an engineering student, would worry when seeing a group of people in the street:

> *I usually deal with this by trying to hurry past them. I make sure I don't look at them in case I draw more attention to myself. If some one bumps into me, I wonder whether they did it deliberately. Ration ally, I know I'm not really in danger, but that doesn't stop me worrying. At a couple of times in my life this sort of thing has even made me a bit reluctant to go out alone, especially at night. If I had to go out, I'd try to make sure a friend was coming with me.*

Just like Ian we may start to withdraw from the situations and people that prompt our suspicions. We may avoid talking about our feelings too: we try to pretend they don't exist. For some people drinking or taking drugs offers a way of blotting out their worries.

Avoiding suspicious thoughts can make us feel better, but the benefit tends to be short term. In the longer run, we can find ourselves having to put a growing amount of energy into avoidance. This means a big increase in the impact that our suspicious thoughts have on our day-today lives. Eventually we can feel trapped by the very worries we're working so hard to avoid.

Treating suspicious thoughts as if they might be correct

Some of us react to suspicious thoughts by treating them as if they might be correct. We fear that people *really might be trying to harm us.* This tends to prompt a range of *safety behaviors* – act ions we take to make it less likely that the threat will actually be carried out.

Common safety behaviors include:

• **Avoiding** the situations in which we feel threatened (in just the sort of way we discussed a little earlier in this chapter).

• If we can't avoid those frightening situations, we might adopt a range of other **defensive tactics** to deal with the perceived threat. For example Chapter 1 looked at Melissa, a 39-year-old mother of three, who felt that a neighbour wanted to break into her house and steal her property. Melissa's response was to make regular checks on her door and window locks and to consider buying a burglar alarm. Similarly, Ian, discussed above, sometimes found that the only way he could face a trip out was by persuading a friend to come too.

• **Trying not to do anything that might provoke or anger** the people we fear. For example, if you're worried about your neighbours, you might try to make as little noise as possible so as not to disturb them. Alice, the lecturer we met earlier in this book, tried to avoid provoking the colleagues she thought were plotting to have her fired by being as friendly as possible at work: *I went on a charm offensive. I laughed at everyone's jokes. I made time to chat with absolutely everyone – even people I really didn't know very well. I'd bring people presents on their birthday. I'd suggest we all went out for drinks or a meal or to the cinema. Heaven knows what people made of all this!* A smaller number of people react in the opposite way. Instead of trying to defuse any potential conflict, they opt for aggression and angrily confront those they think want to do them harm.

• **Seeking help from others** – for example, the police or the local council. Sometimes people pray that God will intervene to save them from potential threat; for other people prayer offers emotional support when they're dealing with persecutory thoughts.

• **Worrying about the perceived threat.** Chapter 1 introduced Liz who suspected that a housemate was trying to steal her possessions and even to poison her. Liz went on to tell us: *I'd* *be thinking about my housemate and what she might have in mind for me all the time. It was the first thing I thought about when I woke up and the last thing in my mind when I went to sleep at night. In between, all day, I'd be worrying. It was my way of stop ping anything bad happening – as if worrying was a way of keeping an eye on my housemate.* For many of us worrying is a form of *vigilance.* If we let our guard down for a moment by thinking about something else, we feel as though we'll be risking the very harm we're trying so hard to avoid.

Trying to understand suspicious thoughts

This is a reaction you're probably familiar with – after all, you're reading this book!

The most common step people take in their bid to find out more about their anxieties is simply to talk about them with other people. They might speak to friends or family, their doc tor or maybe a coun-sellor. Of course, the people you talk to might not be well-placed to advise you on the best ways of dealing with these sorts of worries. But even so, talking to other people about your concerns is almost always worth the trouble. At the very least you get another viewpoint on your ideas. If you're lucky you may also get some reassurance and advice.

There's often another benefit too. The effort involved in explaining your fears to another person can mean that you're expressing those anxieties more fully than you've done before. You also get to hear them out loud. Instead of a jumble of thoughts rattling round your brain, you're presented with some clearer statements of the problem. All this helps give you some perspective on your worries and makes it a little easier for you to assess whether they're justified or not.

Ten of the best (and ten of the worst)

We asked more than a thousand people to identify the most effective strategies for coping with suspicious thoughts. Here are the top ten:

1 Don't see the problem or situation as a threat.
2 See the situation for what it is and nothing more.
3 Try to find the positive side to the situation.
4 Have presence of mind when dealing with the problem or situation.
5 Feel completely clear-headed about the whole thing.
6 Be realistic in your approach to the situation.
7 See the problem as something separate from yourself so you can deal with it.

8 Keep reminding yourself of the good things about yourself.

9 Get things into proportion – nothing is really that important.

10 Just don't take anything personally.

Several of these responses emphasize the importance of *not exaggerating the threat* in any situation. Don't give your suspicious thoughts more attention than they deserve. Instead, try to assess them calmly and realistically. If you think back to the common reactions discussed in the first part of this chapter, you can see that the top ten are generally examples of either ignoring suspicious thoughts or taking a problem-solving approach. What also emerges is the benefit to be gained from *staying positive about yourself.* Don't let suspicious thoughts knock your self-confidence. Don't let them stop you doing the things you like to do. Remember that there *are* people who like and respect you.

Although it doesn't get a mention in the top ten, one other coping strategy stood out from the results of our survey. The people who were most willing to talk about their feelings were the people least likely to be troubled by suspicious thoughts. There's real value in sharing your worries with other people.

Of course the kinds of strategies we've talked about here aren't always easy to put into practice. But they can be learned – and this book will help you to learn them.

You may be wondering which reactions to suspicious thoughts were rated the *least helpful* in our survey. Here's the list:

1 Becoming lonely or isolated.
2 Feeling that no one understands.
3 Feeling worthless and unimportant.
4 Becoming miserable or depressed.
5 Feeling helpless – as if there's nothing you can do about the situation.
6 Criticizing or blaming yourself.
7 Avoiding family or friends.
8 Feeling overpowered and at the mercy of the situation.
9 Stopping doing hobbies or following interests.
10 Daydreaming about times in the past when things were better.

What stands out very clearly in these reactions is how emotional they are. Instead of ignoring the suspicious thoughts or seeing them as a problem to be solved, people feel miserable, worthless, overwhelmed. And when we feel like this, we inevitably cut ourselves off from our family and friends, perhaps in a bid to *avoid* the situations that seem to spark our anxieties. Hobbies no longer interest us. Our world shrinks until it seems that there's only room for our fears.

When we react like this we may wonder whether our suspicious thoughts are actually a sign that we're losing the plot – it can seem as if we're going mad. But, as mentioned earlier in this book, nearly everyone has suspicious thoughts. If having these feelings is a sign of madness then pretty much all of us are in the same boat! So, having suspicious thoughts doesn't mean you're going mad. Far from being an indication of madness, suspicious thoughts are the *understandable* products of the lives we lead and the experiences we've had. Chapters 4 and 5 will look in detail at how suspicious thoughts arise.

Of course, although suspicious thoughts aren't a sign of madness, they can certainly cause considerable distress. For a minority of people these experiences can make them clinically depressed and anxious. As discussed in Chapter 2, suspicious thoughts can sometimes be associated with psychosis, a psychiatric illness. In these cases, professional help may be essential. If you or a loved one is affected in this way you may find the Appendix of this book particularly helpful.

However, these levels of distress are by no means com-mon or inevitable. For the great majority of people it's perfectly possible to get control over suspicious thoughts without seeking professional help. Showing you how is what this book is all about.

Exercise: How do you react to suspicious thoughts?

How do you react to suspicious thoughts? This exercise will give you an indication of your typical responses.

First, think back to a time over the past month when you had a suspicious thought. Tick the box beside the sentence that best describes your reaction. Each sentence is grouped according to the types of reactions we've looked at in this chapter. Try to remember how you felt at the *exact moment* that the thought came to you, rather than how you reacted later. Once you've done this, repeat the exercise for three other times that you've experienced suspicious thoughts.

After you've completed the exercise, ask yourself the following questions:

- Is this how I'd like to react?
- Could I have reacted in other ways?
- What other reactions would have been better for me?

You're only a little way through this book and we've only just begun to outline some positive ways in which you can deal with your suspicious thoughts. But, early as it is, are there any changes you think you could make *now* when you have a suspicious thought? For example could you listen to them less or take a more analytical approach?

Ignoring suspicious thoughts

_ I ignored the thought.
_ I hardly noticed the thought.

_ I felt quite detached from the thought.
_ It didn't really seem to matter.
_ I felt a bit anxious when the thought occurred, but I just carried on with what I was doing.

The problem-solving approach

_ I considered the thought and rejected it.
_ I didn't panic and thought it all through carefully.
_ I thought of all the reasons why the thought couldn't be correct.
_ I wondered what advice my friends would give me.
_ I put the thought into context and instead concentrated on positive things.
_ I decided to see what someone else thought about my anxious feeling.

The emotional response

_ I felt miserable.
_ I felt overwhelmed.
_ I was annoyed with myself.
_ It felt like things were out of control.
_ I felt vulnerable and helpless.
_ I felt ashamed.

Avoiding suspicious thoughts

_ I wanted to withdraw from everybody.

_ I knew that I had to get away from the situation in order to stop the thoughts occurring.

_ I didn't want anyone else to know I'd had the thought.

_ I knew the only way I was going to feel better was by avoiding the thought.

_ I thought that the only way to cope was to have a drink or a smoke.

Treating suspicious thoughts as if they might be correct

_ I believed the thought was probably true and so I needed to get away from the situation.

_ I tried to watch out for the danger.

_ I tried to escape the danger.

_ I was anxious and wanted to get somewhere safe.

_ I wanted to blend in and not upset anyone.

_ I got angry with the people involved.

_ I worried about what was going to happen.

_ I vowed to avoid these situations in future.

Trying to understand suspicious thoughts

_ I knew I had to get more information before deciding what to do.

_ I wanted another perspective on my suspicious thoughts.

_ I thought it was better to be uncertain about what was going on than leap to conclusions.

_ I didn't know what to think but I knew I had to find out more.

CHAPTER SUMMARY

• How we react to suspicious thoughts has a big impact on how well we cope with them.

• Common reactions to suspicious thoughts are to ignore them; to treat them as a problem to be solved; to respond emotionally; to avoid them; to treat them as if they might be correct; to try to understand them.

• The most helpful responses to suspicious thoughts involve keeping them in perspective and not letting them disrupt our lives.

• The least helpful reaction is the emotional response. The thoughts make us miserable and can lead to us withdrawing from normal life.

4

Understanding why paranoid and suspicious thoughts occur

CASE STUDY 1: EMILY' S STORY

(Emily is 34 years old and works as a solicitor. She's married with a two-year-old daughter.)

For quite a while now I've been finding social situations difficult. Sometimes I worry that people are talking about me or laughing at me. Sometimes I feel very distant from the people I'm with – as if I don't belong. From time to time I've felt as if I weren't there at all – like I've somehow vanished. It's been troubling me for a long time, but it seems to have got much worse over the last couple of years. I'm at the stage now where I'm turning down invitations. Staying at home seems a much less stressful option.

I first started having these thoughts just after I left university. Actually, that's probably not quite right. I do remember being at par ties when I was at university and wondering whether people were laughing at me, and there was one girl I suspected might be speaking about me behind my back.

But it was as if the thoughts popped into my head and popped right out again. I never spent any time worrying about them back then.

After I'd finished my law studies I moved to a new city and worked as a trainee solicitor. I found that period quite tough. I'd built up a lot of debt during my studies. I was getting a salary, but it wasn't much. I found the work really exhausting – I was used as a dogsbody, given all the chores no one else wanted to do. I was also convinced I'd made a big mistake in moving to a new city. I didn't know anyone else there and family and friends seemed a very long way away.

I really worried that I'd made the wrong decision taking up law and several times I strongly considered giving it up. There were two reasons why I didn't. First, I didn't want to disappoint my parents: they'd always been so proud that their daughter was going to be a lawyer. The other reason was that I couldn't think of anything else I wanted to do.

It was during this time that I first noticed that I was becoming a little paranoid. The firm that I worked for was a large one – lots of lawyers and lots of social events designed, I think, to test you in subtle, non-legal scenarios. I dreaded these social events and as soon as one was announced I'd start worrying about it. I felt sure I was being judged. I'd see people chatting and if one of the group happened to glance in my direction I was sure it was me they were discussing. And if all that was followed by them laughing – well, that was just awful. I always left as soon as I could and then I'd lie awake replaying the evening in my head.

At one level I knew I was being stupid – that I was imagining things. It was funny because I'd always thought of my dad as being a bit paranoid – he was always fretting about what other people thought of us, always thinking that someone at work had it in for him. I could see that his worries had much more to do with what was going on inside his head than what was actually going on in the real world. But knowing all this didn't make me feel any better.

Things only started to improve when I changed my job. I moved back to London and it was if a huge weight was lifted from me. Suddenly I had a social life again. My family were nearby as well as almost all my friends from school and college. I also felt much more comfortable at work. It was a more relaxed and informal atmosphere than my previous company. We used to go out a lot together after work and I never – or almost never – experienced the kind of worries that I'd had before in social situations.

That all changed around the time I went back to work after maternity leave. I only took three months' leave because I was made to feel, though no one said so openly, that I'd be damaging my career by being away longer. So Lily went to nursery – five days a week. I felt very guilty about this. She was so tiny. I hated leaving her and I worried that I was a terrible mother for doing so. On top of this I had all the usual pressures of work and lots of nights with little sleep. I don't think I've ever felt as tired as I've done over the last eighteen months.

The paranoia reared its head again and this time even worse than before. It got to the stage where I'd avoid going out. I was very close to quitting work. I couldn't face anyone. I knew that if someone so much as glanced at me I'd be worrying about the meaning of that glance for days afterwards. I'd make a mental note of these sorts of 'incidents' while I was out and then analyze them all when I got home, usually while lying awake in bed.

It was crazy. I never told another soul about what I was going through, partly because I was embarrassed that so many people thought I was stupid or not up to scratch in some way. And I thought I had it all figured out: what was there to discuss? It was incredibly lonely though. I missed the social contact; I missed my friends. And I had this awful thing, this secret, that I had to deal with all by myself.

Things only changed when my husband started to doubt my repeated excuses for staying at home. He realized something was wrong, that I *needed to get some help, and from that point on things have got much better.*

CASE STUDY 2: KEITH'S STORY

(Keith is 53 years old, divorced with three daughters and works as a postman).

When my wife and I split up I was sad about it, of course, but I was sure it was the right thing. I was very confident I could cope. I can cook; I know how to keep house. And at first things were fine. I sorted myself out with a nice little flat and enjoyed a bit of time to myself. But it's not worked out the way I thought it would. I feel pretty cut off to tell you the truth. Two of my daughters moved down to London to work so I don't see much of them, and my youngest is a teenager and out and about all the time. The greatest blow was losing both my parents within a year of my divorce. My dad died of a stroke and after that my mum seemed to lose the will to live. We'd always been a very close family. I'd pop in three, four, five times a week. So them passing on was devastating.

Then I began to have a few problems at work. I'd always been happy there, though I'm not all that great with people. I suppose I'm a bit of a loner. I was bullied at school and maybe that's been a factor in not getting on easily with people.

Anyway, the manager moved on and I just didn't hit it off with the guy who replaced him.

He was young and very cocky: thought he knew it all. I think he saw me as a bit of a threat. He also knew that I'd been through a rough time and I think he took advantage of that.

I began to notice that he was treating me differently to everyone else. He'd give me the jobs no one else wanted. He'd ignore me in meetings. If I ever wanted to see him about something, he was always busy. What was really infuriating was the fact that he tried to turn my colleagues against me. I couldn't prove any of it, but I knew that people were starting to treat me differently – people who up until then had been my mates. They'd look at me oddly, or I'd walk into an office and the conversation would suddenly stop. I can think of lots of occasions when I was convinced folk were laughing at me behind my back. I felt that they were always looking to put me down. What before had seemed to be harmless banter now seemed like it was malicious and all aimed at me.

I began to withdraw into myself. I found excuses for not going to the canteen at lunchtime and didn't go to the pub after work much. After a while people stopped asking me, which just confirmed what I was already thinking. I didn't have too much else going on in my life at the time so I had plenty of opportunity to dwell on it all. It became a habit. I'd get home from work, make myself a cup of tea and try to read the pa-

per or have a nap. But then I'd find myself thinking back through the day and then all kinds of things that hadn't bothered me at the time – a comment someone had made, a look I thought someone had given me – started to worry me. I'd go on worrying about them for the rest of the night! It was like I couldn't concentrate on anything else until I'd identified all the ways in which people had tried to get at me that day. I'd be watching the TV and all of a sudden an incident I'd forgotten would come into my head and off I'd go again.

It got to the stage where I dreaded going to work. I slept badly the night before. I could feel myself tensing up on the journey in. By the time I reached the building I was in a right state: heart pounding, headache, sweating – the lot. I had to really fight the temptation to just turn around and go home. Eventually I gave in to that temptation and stayed away altogether. But that didn't help. I was disgusted with myself for giving in to these fears. I felt like I should have been able to deal with the situation. I was sure other people would have handled it much better than me.

I became a bit of a recluse. I didn't go to work and I didn't go out socializing. All day in the house on your own with no one to talk to is hard. You need a reason to get out of bed in the morning, don't you? Mine was usually to check whether anyone from work was outside in the street checking up on me. I got in a stew about my next-door neighbours. I thought they were starting to look at me a bit strangely. If they were noisy at all I used to think they were doing it to get at me. They knew I was having a hard time, so why all the banging and shouting? I don't actually think they were being particularly noisy but that's the way I was seeing things back then.

Introduction

So far in this book we've described the sorts of experiences we're referring to when we use the term 'suspicious thoughts'. We've looked at the events and feelings that can often trigger these thoughts, and we've seen how people usually react to them. But by now you might well be saying to yourself: 'All well and good, but *why* do these kinds of thoughts occur?'

The fact is suspicious thoughts can be caused by several factors and they will vary from person to person. That's the bad news for anyone hoping for a simple answer to the *why* question.

The good news, though, is that there *is* an answer. We *can* make sense of our suspicious thoughts and why they occur. And once we understand our paranoia, we're a long way down the road to coping with it.

Research has identified five main factors involved in the occurrence of suspicious thoughts. All five factors are very common – all of us will have experienced at least some of them. What's important, though, is the way they combine. Suspicious thoughts are caused by a combination of some or all of these five factors:

- Stress and major life changes;
- Emotions (usually negative);
- Internal and external events;
- Our explanations of these internal and external events;
- Reasoning (the way we think things through and come to decisions and judgments).

In the next few pages we'll look in detail at each of these factors and show how they can combine to cause suspicious thoughts and we'll use the stories of Emily and Keith to illustrate the model we're putting together. Of course, as we saw in Chapter 1, the content of suspicious thoughts can vary widely – for example, the type of threat we're worried about and the people we suspect of trying to harm us. But although Emily's and Keith's experiences may not be identical to yours, the ideas and advice we give in the book are relevant to *all* suspicious thoughts, whatever the differences in the details. As you read the following sections, have a think about how the five factors relate to your own experiences and then complete the exercise in section entitled "Exercise: Understanding why your suspicious thoughts occur".

The five factors

1 Stress and major life changes

For many people suspicious thoughts seem to first appear during times of stress and change. You might, for example, be starting a new job or not be getting on with your partner. You may have suffered a bereavement or be finding it hard to make ends meet. For some people taking drugs or drinking too much alcohol can cause stress. The events can be one-offs or carry on over time. What we find stressful is very much a personal thing, of course. However, the stressful experiences that form the background to the development of paranoia often seem to *involve other people.*

Stress, often caused by major life changes, certainly appears to have played a big part in the histories of both Emily and Keith. Emily's first problems with suspicious thoughts occurred when she was a trainee solicitor. She found it hard to get along with colleagues and had few friends locally. She was also suffering under the weight of family expectations: she felt that she *had* to continue with her career, despite all her misgivings, because she didn't want to disappoint her parents. We can see here how many of the stresses affecting Emily involved other people. Added to this for Emily were the pressures of starting a new job and moving to a new city – all of which she had to face on very little sleep and not enough money. No wonder, you might be thinking, she had problems.

It's striking that Emily's suspicious thoughts disappeared as soon as she took herself out of this clearly very difficult situation. They returned, though, at another time of stress and major life change. This time the trigger seems to have been becoming a mother. Becoming a parent for the first time is an exhausting and stressful experience for many people. Added to this for Emily was the struggle to combine work and childcare. Sleeplessness was a major factor again, and it's also noticeable that the pressure of other people's expectations was once more an issue. Emily was forced back to work sooner than she'd like after maternity leave by her worry that her company would punish her for staying away longer.

The roots of Keith's paranoid feelings also lie in a period of great stress. In his case he had to deal with the breakup of his marriage and the isolation which that seems to have brought. The death of his parents followed soon after. These huge life events can hardly have helped Keith deal with the additional challenge of having a new (and perhaps not very likeable) boss.

Stress, then, is the first of the five factors that cause suspicious thoughts. We can illustrate the way these factors combine by means of a simple diagram that we'll build up over the following sections. Here's the first part of the diagram:

> **Stress and major life changes**
> Stressful experiences, for example relationship problems or financial pressures, sleeplessness or shyness.
> Major life changes, such as leaving home or bereavement.

2 Emotions

The sorts of stresses and life changes just discussed often *lead to changes in the way we feel.* They can have a big effect on our emotional state – and really it would be surprising if they didn't. It's inevitable that the death of a friend or relative, money troubles or problems at work are going to have a major impact on our feelings. More often than not, of course, that effect is a negative one. We can feel anxious or depressed. We might become unusually irritable or bad-tempered. We can develop a low opinion of ourselves or others, and sometimes both.

Our emotional state can play a big role in the development of suspicious thoughts. This is because *the way we feel has a big influence on the way we think.* Our emotions affect the way we see ourselves and others. When we're happy we're likely to take a positive view of the world. On the other hand, feeling down is probably going to make us think negatively about things.

Of all our emotions **anxiety** is often very closely linked to the occurrence of suspicious thoughts. That connection isn't in fact all that surprising. Research has shown that anxiety and suspicious thoughts are actually quite similar. In fact, suspicious thoughts can be understood as a type of anxiety.

Let's look at this in a little more detail. Anxiety is all about the anticipation of threat. It's designed to let us know when we might be in danger. Anxiety is our early warning system. It tells us that we need to take action. To use a term discussed in Chapter 2, anxiety makes us aroused.

Anxiety can be a life-saver, but it can also be misleading. Many people feel anxious even when there is no real threat. Some people get anxious at the thought of heights or enclosed spaces. Others worry when they see a dog headed their way, or if they have to take a trip in a plane. It's easy to dismiss these anxieties as irrational phobias but they have their roots in a perfectly sensible awareness of possible danger – after all, falling from a great height is likely to kill you and enclosed spaces can be difficult to get out of. Dogs do very occasionally attack people and from time to time planes do crash. But the truth is that none of these things is very likely. Our anxiety seems *out of proportion* to the reality of the situation.

Anxiety tends to breed more anxiety. When we're anxious we often overestimate the chances of bad things happening to us. We see danger in situations that are actually very safe. We look inwards rather than outwards – we focus on the way we're *fee ling,* rather than making a calm assessment of the world around us.

Given all this, you can see how anxiety can make us worry about the threat from *other people.* We view their behavior as a danger and, looking inward rather than outward, we worry about our suspicions.

Anxiety certainly seems to have played a part in the development of Emily's and Keith's suspicious thoughts. Emily's first experience of paranoid thoughts was tied up with worries about her career choice and with real anxiety about attending social events organized by her employer. When her suspicious thoughts returned it was at a time when Emily was finding it very hard to combine the roles of mother and full-time lawyer and was spending lots of time worrying about her situation. In Keith's case the thought of going to work made him so anxious that it was all he could do to stop himself turning around and heading back home.

But anxiety isn't the only emotion that can lead to suspicious thoughts:

• When we're **sad or depressed or just generally low** we can feel particularly vulnerable, perhaps because we feel different to other people. Something like this seems to have been a factor in Keith's suspicious thoughts. Divorce and the death of his parents had left him feeling very low and very isolated. The fact that Keith had been bullied at school and had felt an outsider throughout his life made him feel especially vulnerable. Keith believed his new manager took advantage of his emotional state to treat him badly and to turn his colleagues against him.

- When we're feeling low we may also feel **guilty or ashamed.** It can seem as if the way things are going for us is actually some sort of **punishment.** We might also believe that other people can see our guilt or shame and will treat us accordingly.

- **Being treated badly by people in the past** can have a lasting effect on the way we feel. This in turn can lead to us thinking that *everyone* is likely to be hostile towards us.

- When we're **angry or irritable** it can seem as if other people are deliberately trying to provoke us. We might well blame others for whatever it is that's making us angry. When we feel like this we tend to be very suspicious about what other people might be up to.

- For a small number of people it's not negative emotions (unhappiness, anxiety, anger) that lead to suspicious thoughts. Rather, it's feelings of great **happiness.** They feel great about themselves and wonder why other people don't seem to share their opinion. It can seem as if they haven't had the recognition or rewards they deserve and they may suspect that this is because of the hostile actions of other people.

Your emotions can change constantly, of course. Whatever stresses and strains you may be under, you're not necessarily anxious or depressed or irritable all the time. In the same way, suspicious thoughts may come and go.

That said, it's clear that *our emotional state plays a significant part in the development of suspicious thoughts.* The difficult situations that all of us have to deal with at some point in our lives can lead to feelings of anxiety, depression, anger and guilt. When you feel like this you can find yourself worrying that other people are out to harm you.

Let's build this second factor into the diagram we began in section entitled "Stress and major life changes":

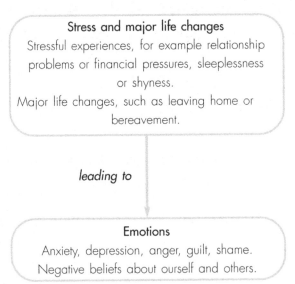

Stress and major life changes
Stressful experiences, for example relationship problems or financial pressures, sleeplessness or shyness.
Major life changes, such as leaving home or bereavement.

leading to

Emotions
Anxiety, depression, anger, guilt, shame.
Negative beliefs about ourself and others.

3 Internal and external events

Chapter 2 looked at how suspicious thoughts are often triggered by the situations we encounter in the world and by the way we feel inside. These are called external and internal triggers.

Common **external triggers** are:

- Social situations;
- Situations from which it's difficult to escape;
- Unusual events, coincidences and apparent connections;
- Being alone;
- Feeling exposed;
- Situations in which we think we might be blamed, accused, mocked or criticized; and
- Ambiguous verbal and non-verbal signs.

Common **internal triggers** are:

- Our emotions;
- Feelings of arousal;
- Changes in the way we perceive the world (anomalous experiences); and
- Taking drugs or drinking excessive amounts of alcohol.

These experiences form the third factor in the development of suspicious thoughts and they're hugely important. Suspicious thoughts don't spring from nowhere: they're the result of our attempts to make sense of the way we feel and the things that happen to us. Often these events and feelings can seem very ambiguous: it's hard to know exactly what's going on. As well as being ambiguous they can often also be quite negative – enjoyable experiences don't seem as likely to lead to a paranoid interpretation.

In Emily's case her suspicious thoughts were triggered the first time around by company social situations and later by almost any form of contact with other people. She'd spend hours analyzing all the ambiguous verbal and non-verbal signs she'd encountered: for example, glances and comments and smiles. As we saw in the previous section, Emily was also dealing with feelings of anxiety, unhappiness and guilt – all typical internal triggers. To these we can add the fact that she was badly down on her sleep caused the first time around by overwork and then later by overwork combined with the nighttime habits of a small baby. Sleeplessness is a common cause of the sort of altered perception of the world we call anomalous experiences. One form her anomalous experiences took was *depersonalization* – the feeling that we don't really exist. Emily would feel this way sometimes at parties.

For Keith too there were strong internal and external triggers for his paranoid thoughts. We know that the death of his parents and the break-up of his marriage had left him feeling very down. We've also seen how anxious the thought of work eventually made him. His anxiety put him in a state of arousal, the term used to describe a state of heightened sensitivity to the world around us, and in particular to its possible dangers. Added to these internal triggers was the external one of simply going to work, something that for years had been straightforward for him but now with a change of manager had become extremely stressful.

One possible trigger that we haven't yet mentioned is family background. Emily describes her father's suspicious thoughts and sees her own behavior as very similar to his. Can our genes make us more or less likely to experience suspicious thoughts? Unfortunately, the research needed to answer this question hasn't yet been done but certainly we all learn ways of thinking and acting from our parents and other close family members. If they see other people as a source of danger then it's very possible that we pick up this behavior from them.

Our diagram of the five factors producing suspicious thoughts is taking shape. The pattern is generally this: stress leads to changes in our emotions, often making us anxious or worried or depressed. When we feel like this we take much more notice of the way we feel and the situations we encounter. Sometimes these internal and external events are the *product* of our changed emotional state.

4 Our explanations of internal and external events

Stress and major life changes
Stressful experiences, for example relationship problems or
financial pressures, sleeplessness or shyness.
Major life changes, such as leaving home or bereavement.

leading to

Emotions
Anxiety, depression, anger, guilt, shame.
Negative beliefs about ourself and others.

*producing or causing
us to notice*

Internal and external events
Ambiguous or negative events, often involving other people.
Emotional feelings, anomalous experiences, arousal.

If the internal and external events outlined above are the third factor in the development of suspicious thoughts, the fourth is our attempt to *explain* these experiences.

It's perfectly natural to try to understand the world around us and the way we feel inside. But when we're stressed and feeling low or anxious or irritable our explanations are likely to be fairly negative. We think the worst – and often we think the worst of people around us. It can seem as if the odd or unpleasant things we've been experiencing are caused by other people. And because it's so difficult to know what anyone else is really thinking, it's all too easy to come to this conclusion. A comment from someone that wouldn't prompt a second thought when we're feeling happy can seem worryingly significant when we're stressed. We agonize for hours about what it might mean – worry that we'd be spared if there were some way to know for certain what the other person really intended.

> **Stress and major life changes**
> Stressful experiences, for example relationship problems or financial pressures, sleeplessness or shyness.
> Major life changes, such as leaving home or bereavement.

leading to

> **Emotions**
> Anxiety, depression, anger, guilt, shame.
> Negative beliefs about ourself and others.

producing or causing us to notice

> **Internal and external events**
> Ambiguous or negative events, often involving other people.
> Emotional feelings, anomalous experiences, arousal.

leading to

> **Our explanation of events**
> Searching for understanding; worrying about what events mean.

Both Emily and Keith spent long periods worrying about the various external and internal events that they experienced (and which were described in the preceding section).

I'd make a mental note of these sorts of 'incidents' while I was out and then analyze them all when I got home.

(Emily)

I'd find myself thinking back through the day and then all kinds of things that hadn't bothered me at the time – a comment someone had made, a look I thought someone had given me – started to worry me.

(Keith)

Both came to believe that the incidents bothering them could be explained by *the hostile actions of other people.* Instead of saying to themselves 'I'm really stressed at the moment – really uptight and upset; I need time to sort myself out', they decided they were under threat from others.

Our diagram of the five factors producing suspicious thoughts is nearly complete.

5 Reasoning

The fifth and final part of the puzzle is *reasoning,* the term used to describe the way we think things through and come to decisions and judgments.

Research has shown that it's much more likely that we'll have suspicious thoughts – and those thoughts are likely to go on for longer and cause us more distress – if we do any of the following things:

- **Have a need for certainty.** As we've discussed, it's natural to want to understand our experiences, especially if they are the sort of odd and unsettling experiences people often have during periods of great stress and emotional disturbance. But being able to live with uncertainty, accepting our experiences without feeling the need to worry about what they mean, makes it much less likely that we'll develop suspicious thoughts. This is easier said than done, of course. It can be a big relief to think that we have an explanation, even if that explanation isn't a very happy one. Certainly, Keith and Emily were both determined to know what each of the small incidents that troubled them really meant.

- **Blaming others.** We usually explain events in one of three ways. Events can be caused by ourselves, by the situation or by other people. For example, if you're late for work you could blame yourself for not getting up earlier; or you could put the blame on the traffic congestion that means it can be hard to get anywhere on time; or you could blame the other commuters who pushed in front of you in the queue for a train ticket or took the last place on the bus. If we tend to see other people as the cause of events (psychologists call this *making external attributions),* we're much more likely to have suspicious thoughts.

  • **Jumping to conclusions.** A decision or judgment made quickly isn't always going to be a mistake, but in general it's better to think through a situation carefully first. When we're anxious we often rush to a decision, basing our decision on only a little bit of data. It's hard to take the time to think things through or gather more evidence when we're worried or afraid. But if we don't take the time to gather and analyze the evidence for our thoughts and feelings, and if we don't talk things over with other people, we run the risk of jumping to the wrong conclusion – and that wrong conclusion may well be that other people are out to hurt us.

  Emily, for example, sometimes jumped to the conclusion that she was being discussed on the basis of just one piece of possible evidence – other people's glances: *If one of the group happened to glance to my direction, that was it: I was sure it was me they were discussing.* Emily didn't investigate any further: she didn't, for example, go over to the group to hear what they were chatting about. The same is true of Keith. He didn't take the time to think things through: *as soon as something happened I didn't like, I tended to just assume the worst.*

• **Not considering alternative explanations.** Sometimes suspicious thoughts are just the first thing that comes to mind when we're thinking about experiences that we've had. But those suspicious thoughts can really take hold if we don't try to think of alternative explanations for those experiences. Emily, for example, didn't consider the possibility that her conclusions might have been wrong: *I thought I had it all figured out. What was there to discuss?*

Some experiences (hallucinations, for example) can be so disturbing and so difficult to explain that it's hard to come up with alternative explanations. But you're much less likely to be troubled by suspicious thoughts if you're able to think beyond your first paranoid reaction – if you can keep in mind that what you've seen or what you feel can be explained in other ways. It might be a question of remembering that you're feeling a bit stressed or down and reminding yourself of the effect that can have on the way you see the world. It's these alternative explanations, these ways of seeing past our initial reaction to events, that this book sets out to provide.

With this fifth factor, our model of how suspicious thoughts are caused is finally complete.

Exercise: Understanding why your suspicious thoughts occur

This chapter has presented the five factors that combine to cause suspicious thoughts, and we've illustrated this using a simple flow diagram. Think about your own suspicious thoughts and then fill in the blank diagram below using your own experiences. To help you get started you will find below a list of typical examples that fall under each of the five factors.

Stress and major life changes

- Problems with friends.
- Problems with work colleagues.
- Problems with your partner.
- Not getting on with people.
- Being bullied.
- Leaving home.
- Becoming isolated from other people.
- Starting a new job.
- Problems in the family.
- Bereavement.
- Work pressures.
- Financial pressures.
- Failing (or feeling as if you've failed) at something.

Stress and major life changes
Stressful experiences, for example relationship problems or
financial pressures, sleeplessness or shyness.
Major life changes, such as leaving home or bereavement.

leading to

Emotions
Anxiety, depression, anger, guilt, shame.
Negative beliefs about ourself and others.

producing or causing
us to notice

Internal and external events
Ambiguous or negative events, often involving other people.
Emotional feelings, anomalous experiences, arousal.

leading to

Our explanation of events
Searching for understanding; worrying about
what events mean.

influenced by

Reasoning
Needing certainty; blaming others: jumping to conclusions:
not considering alternative explanations for events.

leading to

Suspicious thoughts

- A traumatic event.
- Physical, emotional or sexual abuse.
- Being assaulted.

- Going without sleep.
- Taking drugs or too much alcohol.

Emotions

Anxiety

- Feeling fearful.
- Feeling nervous.
- Expecting the worst.
- Overestimating the chances of the threat occurring.
- Feeling worried.
- Feeling as if things are out of control.
- Focusing on the way you're feeling.
- Worrying about what other people have planned for you.

Lowered mood

- Feeling miserable or sad.
- Feeling vulnerable.
- Feeling as if you're different to other people.
- Feeling guilty.
- Feeling ashamed.
- Believing that you deserve to be harmed.
- Believing that you're powerless.
- Feeling frightened of rejection by others.

- Dwelling on things.

Anger

- Feeling angry or irritable.
- Feeling tense.
- Feeling as if you're on a short fuse.
- Resenting other people.
- Worrying about what other people might be doing to you.

Elation

- Feeling overjoyed.
- Feeling as if you're special.
- Believing you're exceptionally talented.
- Feeling your thoughts race.

Internal and external events

Non-verbal signs

- Facial expressions.
- The look in people's eyes.
- Hand gestures.
- Laughter and smiles.
- Whistling and shouting.

Verbal signs

- Snatches of conversation.
- Coincidences.
- Feeling aroused.
- Feeling that things are unusually significant.

Anomalous experiences

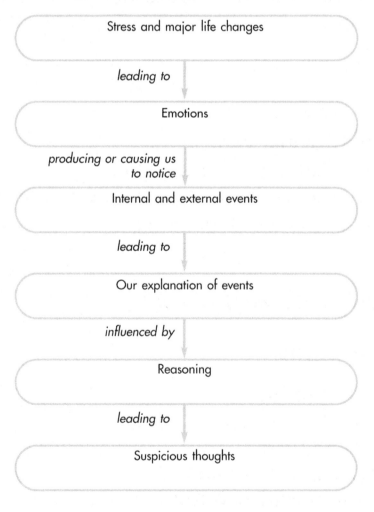

- Things appear brighter or more vivid.
- Sounds seem louder and more intrusive.
- Being unusually sensitive to smells.
- Objects seem odd to the touch.
- Feeling as if you're not really there, or that other people aren't really there.
- Illusions and hallucinations.
- Being easily startled.
- Having trouble concentrating.

Your explanation of events

- Wanting to make sense of events.
- Trying to figure things out.
- Worrying about what's going on.
- Dwelling on things.

Reasoning

- Feeling relieved that you know what's going on.
- Jumping to conclusions.
- Tending to see events as being caused by other people.
- Not discussing your thoughts and feelings with others.

- Not weighing up the evidence for your worries.
- Not considering that you might be mistaken.
- Not considering alternative explanations for your experiences.

CHAPTER SUMMARY

- There's no single reason why we experience suspicious thoughts.
- Suspicious thoughts are usually the result of a combination of five factors:
  - Stress and major life changes;
  - Our emotions;
  - Internal and external events;
  - Our interpretation of these events;
  - Our reasoning – the way we think things through and come to decisions and judgments.

5

Understanding why suspicious thoughts persist and why they cause distress

Introduction

As we saw in the previous chapter, suspicious thoughts are usually caused by a combination of factors. If you are having to deal with a stressful situation, this will have an impact on the way you feel: you might become anxious or depressed, for example. When we feel like this, we notice things that normally we'd not give a second thought to but that now seem odd or confusing. When we try to make sense of these odd events, we come to the conclusion that other people are out to harm us.

Everyone has suspicious thoughts from time to time. Often they can be shrugged off almost without us taking any notice; some times they can take hold and cause real problems. This chapter shows why some suspicious thoughts keep coming back to us and why they cause us distress. As we'll see, it's really a question of how we react to these thoughts.

Chapter 3 looked at the variety of ways in which people react to suspicious thoughts: some helpful, some not so helpful. Here we're going to concentrate on four of the least helpful ones:

- Believing that our suspicions may be true;
- Behaving as if our suspicions are true;
- Feeling anxious;
- Feeling down.

Research has shown that it's these four responses that determine how long our suspicious thoughts last and how badly they affect us.

Four key responses

1 Believing that our suspicions may be true

How many thoughts do you have every day? Hundreds, certainly; thousands, quite possibly. If your thoughts are anything like ours, then most of them will come and go almost without you noticing – which may be just as well!

Out of this jumble of thoughts the ones that stand out are often emotional: you may remember thinking how infuriating the noise made by your neighbours was, for example, or how happy you felt to see your friends at a party. Suspicious thoughts are also more likely to make an impression on us.

It's one thing to remember the suspicious thoughts that popped into our head that day, but once we start *believing* them, or thinking that they *may* be true, the following two things tend to happen:

• We start to notice the things that seem to confirm our suspicions and fail to notice the things that don't. Psychologists call this the *belief confirmation bias.*

• Because we believe our suspicious thoughts we stop considering *alternative explanations* for events.

The belief confirmation bias is hardly surprising: it's very natural and very common. Almost all of us are generally more comfortable with the things we know and understand and that fit our view of the world than we are with those things that challenge our preconceptions. As long ago as the seventeenth century, the philosopher Francis Bacon wrote:

The human understanding when it has once adopted an opinion ... draws all things else to support and agree with it. And though there be a greater number and weight of instances to be found on the other side, yet these it either neglects and despises, or else by some distinction sets aside and rejects.

We can see the belief confirmation bias at work in the experiences of both Emily and Keith. For Emily social situations are opportunities for other people to do her down. All that she can remember about them are the apparently ambiguous glances, comments or smiles that she thinks are being direct- ed at her. Social contact seems to Emily to be just a smokescreen for hostility. Any friendly behavior makes no impression at all on her. There's a very dramatic contrast between this and Emily's attitude to social occasions at happier times of her life.

In a similar way Keith's view of his colleagues at work focuses exclusively on the ways in which he believes they're getting at him. And something very interesting happens. Keith's suspicions influence his thinking so much that behavior that he used to find harmless now seems quite the opposite: *What before had seemed to be harmless banter now seemed like it was malicious and all aimed at me.*

The drive to find incidents that confirm Keith's suspicious thoughts is so strong that it completely changes his reaction to the world around him.

Just like Emily and Keith when we start to be- lieve our suspicious thoughts we notice all the things that seem to confirm our fears and none of the things that don't. We're so determined to find the evidence to prove our suspicions are correct that we put the worst possible interpretation on events. If we do come across friendly behavior we're likely to dismiss or distrust it rather than doubt our suspicious thoughts. So, for example, the banter at the office becomes for Keith a joke at his expense when not long before he'd found it enjoyable. In a similar way, we might interpret a friendly gesture from a neighbour, friend or family member we're suspicious about as just a way to get us off our guard.

The belief confirmation bias can be the start of a vicious cycle: the more evidence we find for our suspicions, the more we believe them. The more we believe our suspicious thoughts, the less likely it is that we'll take seriously – or even notice – anything that seems to disprove them.

In a very similar way the more we believe that our suspicious thoughts might be true, the less likely we are to consider *alternative explanations* for the events that are worrying us. As we've seen in previous chapters it's often difficult to know for certain what people really mean by a comment or an action. Say, for example, that you pass someone you know from work in the street. You smile at them but they don't smile back. In fact, they don't acknowledge you at all. There are lots of possible explanations for this behavior:

- They didn't see you because they weren't wearing their glasses.
- They were lost in their own thoughts.

- They're not good at recognizing people out of context. They would have noticed you at work because that's where they'd expect to meet you.
- They ignored you because they don't like you.
- They're shy in social situations and try to avoid them.

Any of these scenarios could be true and there are probably many more possibilities. But if we're feeling suspicious, we're likely to focus on only one explanation: we assume our colleague ignored us deliberately because she doesn't like us.

Emily and Keith spend lots of time worrying about other people's behavior, but neither of them is able to see beyond their suspicions. For Emily the situation is straightforward: her colleagues are out to do her down *(I thought I had it all figured out)*. Keith, too, is absorbed in his anxieties:

It was like I couldn't concentrate on anything else until I'd identified all the ways in which people had tried to get at me that day.

Neither Keith nor Emily seriously considers that the behavior that worries them so much could be explained in lots of different ways, most of which aren't worrying at all. Emily, for example, would see a group of people chatting at a social function. If one of them happened to glance in her direction, she would decide that they were talking about her. Well, that's a possible explanation for what was going on, but there are plenty of other possibilities. The group may have been discus sing someone or something entirely different. If by some chance Emily was the topic of conversation the comments might have been positive – perhaps someone was saying how impressed she'd been with her work. The man glancing in Emily's direction may have been looking at someone else, or just looking around the room. He may not even have spotted Emily. If he did see her, his feelings toward her may have been friendly. Perhaps he would have liked her to join the conversation.

You can doubtless imagine other possible explanations. What's so striking is that Emily doesn't seem to consider any of them. Her suspicious thoughts are so powerful that *she focuses only on the explanation that confirms her fears.*

2 Behaving as if our suspicions are true

Once we start *thinking* there's some truth in our suspicions we start *behaving* differently too. Here are three common ways in which we change the way we behave:

- We adopt safety behaviors.
- We act differently when we're with other people.
- We don't try to sort out difficult relationships.

One of the most common reactions to suspicious thoughts is to adopt safety behaviors. As Chapter 3 discussed, safety behaviors are actions we take to make it less likely that the threat we fear will actually be carried out. The most common type of safety behavior is avoiding the situations in which we feel threatened – psychologists call this *avoidance.* For example, if you're worried about being attacked you might avoid going out side or to particular parts of town. But there are other types of safety behaviors. You might only go into a situation you feel is threatening with somebody you trust. You may try to please the people you think are out to get you (this is called *appeasement).* Or you might try to protect yourself by keeping constantly on your guard.

It's perfectly natural to try to avoid danger. But one of the consequences of safety behaviors is that it then becomes very hard to know whether we really were *in danger.* For instance, Keith felt that by staying away from work he was avoiding trouble with his boss and colleagues. He assumed that his suspicions were accurate and changed his behavior accordingly. But by doing so he also missed the opportunity to find out whether any trouble was actually going to occur. After all, he might have been pleasantly surprised.

So *safety behaviors rob us of the chance to test our fears.* And if we never get to test whether our anxieties are true we can all too easily become locked into them. As Keith and Emily both experienced, avoiding worrying situations can all too easily lead to isolation. We tend to withdraw from social contact and become less active – both Keith and Emily eventually stopped seeing other people altogether. We end up with lots of time on our hands, time we're likely to spend dwelling on our fears.

Suspicious thoughts can also change the way we act when we're with certain people. Instead of relaxing and enjoying their company we worry about the threat they might pose to us. Often these kinds of feelings make us seem preoccupied, nervous and withdrawn. We might seem timid or secretive. Some people, on the other hand, become angry and upset. Not surprisingly, when we feel this way we're unlikely to be good company. To other people it seems like we're just not ourselves – and of course we're not: our normal self is buried beneath our suspicions.

Unfortunately, as Keith's experience shows, this change in the way we act when we're with other people has negative consequences:

> *I withdrew into myself a bit – I found excuses for not going to the canteen at lunchtime and didn't go to the pub after work much. So people stopped asking me, which was probably understandable but didn't make me feel any better: it just confirmed what I was already thinking.*

It's another vicious cycle. Our suspicions make us difficult to be around, so after a while our friends and colleagues stop trying to spend time with us. This appears to provide even more justification for our suspicions: it seems like people really don't like us.

Chapter 4 looked at how suspicious thoughts often have at their root stressful experiences. Difficult relationships, whether it be with a partner, a family member, a friend or a colleague, are a prime example of these stressful experiences. Keith's anxieties, for example, seemed to have their roots in the break-up of his marriage, his increasingly distanced relationship with his children and his unhappy dealings with his manager. It's hard enough at the best of times to talk openly with someone about problems in your relationship. It's even harder when you're having suspicious thoughts about that other person. Instead of starting a dialogue about the issues that need resolving, we're likely to turn inwards and brood on our worries just as Keith did. Keith saw very little of his ex-wife and his children, and he was unwilling or unable to talk to his manager about the tension he felt between them. He became isolated, alone with his anxieties:

> I didn't have too much else going on in my life at the time so I had plenty of opportunity to dwell on it all.

Once again, we can see a familiar pattern emerging. Keith's stressful relationships helped produce suspicious thoughts. The suspicious thoughts made it almost impossible for Keith to have the kind of open discussions with his ex-wife or children or boss that might have improved these relationships. Instead, Keith retreated into himself, the relationships got no better and the suspicious thoughts were reinforced. It can be difficult to break out of this cycle.

3 Feeling anxious

We've seen how suspicious thoughts are caused by an emotional response to stressful experiences. Of all the emotions anxiety is the one that seems to be most closely linked to the development of suspicious thoughts.

But anxiety isn't just an important factor in the *creation* of suspicious thoughts, it also helps determine how long those thoughts *continue* and how badly they *affect* us. Suspicious thoughts can often be very upsetting. The feelings of threat and danger they provoke are so strong that they make us anxious – after all, the purpose of anxiety is specifically to alert us to possible danger. These new feelings of anxiety only intensify our suspicious thoughts, which then in turn increase our anxiety, and so on. It's yet another vicious cycle.

Emily's experiences provide a revealing example of this. Her second spell of suspicious thoughts came at a time when she was struggling to balance the demands of being a parent and of a demanding and highly pressured job. She was gripped by anxiety both about her competence as a mother and as a lawyer. She worried that trying to combine work and motherhood was unfair to her daughter; and she feared that her career could be damaged if colleagues thought she was prioritizing her family over her work.

The suspicious thoughts she began to have about her colleagues only increased her anxiety:

> *I knew that if someone so much as glanced at me, I'd be worrying about the meaning of that glance for days afterwards.*

Emily broods on her suspicions, turning them over and over in her mind. But as we've seen already, becoming absorbed in worries only seems to increase them. When we can't get any perspective on our anxieties, we can become locked into them: anxiety breeds anxiety. Emily's fears escalate to the point where she is unwilling to leave the house, and on the verge of quitting the job that she has worked so hard to keep.

For some people worrying can actually be a form of safety behavior (have a look back in section entitled "Treating suspicious thoughts as if they might be correct" for more on this). Worrying keeps us alert and ready to deal with the danger. We feel that, if we stop being anxious, we'll be letting down our guard and become suddenly vulnerable. In fact, all that this sort of constant worrying achieves is to keep us focused on our suspicious thoughts. And if our suspicions are rooted in bad experiences we've had in the past, worrying can revive our memories of those experiences. Sometimes we start to worry that our anxiety is a sign that we're losing control. This is called *worry about worry* and it's something Emily experienced:

When I thought about the effect my paranoia was having on my life, I began to wonder whether I might be going a bit mad.

4 Feeling down

Just like anxiety, feeling down is an emotion that can both help cause suspicious thoughts and be a major factor in keeping them going.

Suspicious thoughts can frequently make us feel sad and miserable. And the lower we feel, the longer our suspicious thoughts are likely to stick around. Here are some common ways in which our suspicions can depress us:

• We feel out of control, as if we're powerless to shake off our worries. We can even start to fear, as Emily did, that we're going mad.

• Our suspicious thoughts can awaken all kinds of negative feelings we've had all along about ourselves. This was the case with Emily: *I'd worry that, because I couldn't join in with a conversation, the others would think I was stupid. I'd think: I don't belong here. I don't fit in ... That feeling of not belonging, of being different and isolated, is actually something I've experienced at various times of my life.*

• Keith's struggle to deal with his suspicious thoughts reinforced his sense of inadequacy: *I was disgusted with myself for giving in to these fears. I felt like I should have been able to deal with the situation. I was sure other people would have handled it much better than me.* Sometimes we can have such a low opinion of our selves that we feel we *deserve* to be punished or harmed.

• Our negative views about the world around us can seem confirmed: people are cruel, life is unfair, the world is dangerous.

These kinds of feelings make us all the more receptive to our suspicions: our fears seem more convincing than ever. As a result they're also likely to stay with us for longer.

One more very important thing can happen when we feel down: we have much less energy for anything other than worrying. We withdraw into ourselves, stop socializing and generally reduce our activity levels. Both Keith and Emily ended up retreating from the world:

> *I became a bit of a recluse. I didn't go to work and I didn't go out socializing*

> (Keith).

> *It got to the stage where I'd avoid going out. I just didn't feel up to it. I was very close to quitting work. I couldn't face anyone. I think I was just exhausted*

(Emily).

But doing less means worrying more. With no work or hobbies or social contact, there's really nothing else to keep us busy. Think about your own experiences: when you're busy doing something (and particularly something you enjoy), do you have more or fewer suspicious thoughts? Nine times out of ten you'll find that you have far fewer suspicious thoughts.

Some conclusions

We've seen that the way we respond to our suspicious thoughts decides how long a period of time those thoughts linger and how much distress they cause us. The more we do any of the following the more prolonged and severe our experience is likely to be:

- Believe that our suspicions may be true.
- Behave as if our suspicions are true.
- Feel anxious.
- Feel down.

These four key responses and their relationship to suspicious thoughts are shown in the diagram on the next page.

Believing our suspicions are true
Noticing the things that seem to confirm our suspicions and failing to notice those that don't: the belief confirmation bias.
Failing to consider alternative explanations for events.

Behaving as if our suspicions are true
Adopting safety behaviors (for example, avoiding situations).
Acting differently around other people.
Not trying to improve difficult relationships.

Suspicious thoughts

Feeling anxious
Feeling worried.
Becoming focused on ourselves and our worries.
Worrying about our worries; feeling as if things are gettingout of control.

Feeling down
Feeling miserable, sad or depressed.
Feeling powerless.
Thinking we deserve to be threatened.
Feeling negative about ourselves and the world around us.
Becoming inactive.

The way suspicious thoughts affect people is often self-perpetuating, as we've seen in the pages above. For example, they can make you feel anxious, which increases your suspicious thoughts, which in turn makes you even more anxious. We've tried to show this vicious cycle in the diagram by making the arrows point in both directions indicating how thoughts, feelings and behavior all affect each other.

Exercise: Understanding why your suspicious thoughts keep coming back to you and why they cause distress

For this exercise think about some specific recent instances when you have had suspicious or paranoid thoughts. Describe what you did or how you behaved in the blank diagram below. To get you thinking, we've provided below, some examples of common ways of behaving that fall into each of the four typical responses to suspicious thoughts.

Believing our suspicions are true

_ I'm good at noticing things that seem to support my suspicious thoughts.

_ I'm not good at noticing things that seem to contradict my suspicious thoughts.

_ I always jump to a negative interpretation of events.

_ I'm not good at thinking through the range of possible explanations for an event.

Behaving as if our suspicions are true

_ I try to avoid situations in which I feel threatened.

_ I try to get away from difficult situations.

_ I tend to spend less time out with other people.

_ I'm often looking to other people for protection.

_ I often think I've only managed to avoid a threatening situation by the skin of my teeth.

_ I prefer being on my own.

_ I'm often irritable with people.

_ I'm quite secretive.

_ I find it hard to have a relaxed conversation with someone.

_ If I have a problem with someone I don't feel comfortable trying to talk it through with them.

Feeling anxious

_ My suspicious thoughts make me anxious.

_ I spend a lot of time worrying about things.

_ I try to always be prepared for danger.

_ Most of the time I'm thinking about myself and my worries.

_ Sometimes it seems as if my suspicious thoughts are getting out of control.

_ Bad memories keep coming to mind.

Feeling down

_ I generally feel quite sad.

_ I often feel powerless.

_ I think that I deserve to be harmed.

_ I believe the world is a cruel and unfair place.

_ I don't get as much enjoyment out of life as I used to.

_ I do less than I used to.

– I'm a lot more passive these days – I'm more likely to spend time watching TV than going out or doing things around the house.

130

– Feeling down.

PART TWO

Overcoming Suspicious Thoughts

6

The beginnings of change

Introduction

Already you've come a long way. By working through the past five chapters you're much further forward in your understanding of what suspicious thoughts are, why they occur and why they can cause us such problems. Over the next three chapters we'll build on this progress with six practical steps you can take to overcome your suspicious thoughts.

We can't solve a problem unless we understand it. How else would we know where to start and what to do? So the first of the practical steps (the two covered in this chapter) are designed to help you really understand your *own* suspicious thoughts. You'll be moving on from the more general understanding of paranoia you've gained from the first half of this book to develop a detailed awareness of how and when these thoughts affect you. We want you to take a step back from your anxieties and instead become an *observer* of them.

But before we get started properly on these practical steps, let's first look at some positive behaviors and attitudes that will help you succeed.

The foundations of success

I have understood that it takes time to put all the pieces together, countless hours on the range and in front of a mirror. You are teaching your body to do new things, so you start with 'Can I hit ten balls on the range like I need to?' Then you play nine holes with your buddies and do what you aim to for only four holes, then you do it for a round. Then you do it in a tournament for two days, then for four days, then you have to know you can do it in a major down the stretch. And all of a sudden it comes together.

Tiger Woods

I knew I was stronger than I've ever been, but it's what goes on in your head that counts.

Kelly Holmes

Goals need to be tackled with the right attitude. The quotation from Olympic gold medalist Kelly Holmes expresses this truth beautifully. Sports stars know that what sets champions apart is not so much their natural ability, but the mindset they adopt in order to maximize that ability. A positive mindset is the springboard for positive behavior.

Some sports people have an instinctive feel for this mindset, but most have to learn it and then work to make it second nature. We can all learn these good mental habits. They're use ful for everyone, not just athletes. They can certainly play a big role in helping us to deal with suspicious thoughts. Remember: *it's what goes on in your head that counts.* As you work on the six steps we present over the next three chapters, see if you can adopt the following positive habits:

• Make sure you **set regular time aside** to work with this book. If you want to make progress with anything it's so much easier if you work at it on a regular basis and not just when you happen to feel like it. We suggest you spend 20 minutes every day, or perhaps every other day, reading this book and trying out the exercises and techniques in it. It's a good idea to schedule this time in your diary. It's all too easy to let other commitments crowd out the things we want to do for ourselves; but no one likes missing an appointment – even an appointment with yourself!

• Take it **one step at a time.** Don't rush – as the great golfer Tiger Woods says, it takes time to put all the pieces together. Stick to your guns, even if you feel like you're not making progress as fast as you'd like: you'll get there in the end. We like the quotation from Tiger Woods that introduces this section because it shows how methodically and pa-tiently he has worked to improve his game. He takes it a step at a time, setting small targets and gradually building up to the kind of performance he's looking for: 'all of a sudden it comes together'.

- **Be willing to try things out.** Change is often difficult. Most of us are more comfortable with what we're used to than with new things – and especially new ideas. But just by reading this book you've already shown that you're interested in turning things around. Try to approach the various suggestions we make with an open mind, no matter how crazy they might seem.

- **Back yourself to succeed.** Build your self-confidence by encouragement and rewards. Criticism is rarely good for motivation. Being hard on yourself will just make you feel worse. It will put you in exactly the *wrong* frame of mind to take on any sort of challenge. If your attempt to deal with your suspicious thoughts isn't going as well or as fast as you'd like, try not to blame yourself. Stay positive, remember the progress you've made (you've made it this far in our book, for one thing), and encourage yourself to push on to success. Make sure you reward yourself when you've completed a task. If you've tried out one of the techniques we suggest, treat yourself – buy that CD or box of chocolates. And feel good about yourself.

- **Monitor your efforts.** Sports people often watch videos of their performances so that they can get a more objective sense of their strengths and weaknesses. Of course, videoing yourself probably isn't going to be an option, but you can still maintain a very good record of your efforts by writing them down. Keep a small notebook handy and jot down what you do from this book, what you learn and how you feel. It will help you gain the distance you need to think clearly about your experiences. And over time it will also show you just how much progress you've made.

• **Set achievable goals.** One of the authors of this book (you'll have to guess which one) enjoys playing golf, but would also like to be a lot better at it. However, no matter how doggedly he sticks to these principles, no matter how hard he tries, he's never going to be able to play golf like Tiger Woods. His game will improve, that's for sure, but no way near enough to win an open championship. Obviously, if our mystery golfer has his heart set on challenging Tiger Woods, he's going to be bitterly disappointed. Despite all his efforts, his objective just isn't realistic. On the other hand, a goal to significantly improve his game is one that's within his grasp – and one he can feel proud about achieving.

It's very important that you set yourself achievable goals. If you don't you are probably setting yourself up for certain failure. We often meet people who desperately want never to feel paranoid again. This is completely understandable given the distress and problems that suspicious thoughts have caused them. But we always explain that what they'd like to achieve just isn't possible. Everyone has suspicious thoughts from time to time, just as everyone is sometimes sad or anxious. None of us can hope to be happy all the time – unhappiness is part of life. It's just the same with suspicious thoughts. Human beings are social creatures; we live surrounded by other people. It's inevitable that occasionally we'll wonder what other people are up to.

You might aim to make your suspicious thoughts occur less often. You might try to make them less upsetting. And you might want to stop them getting in the way of your social life or hobbies. All these objectives are within your grasp. But preventing your suspicious thoughts from *ever* occurring again is unrealistic. You would be setting yourself a goal that no one can achieve. When you do have a suspicious thought – and eventually you're bound to – you'll feel disappointed, frustrated and ashamed.

Avoiding this feeling of failure is actually quite simple: choose goals you can expect to achieve. When you're deciding which goals to set yourself, start by thinking about the effect suspicious thoughts have on you. It's best to ground your goals in your experiences, rather than picking something fantastic but unrealistic or something that might be right for someone else but isn't really relevant to you. So if you find your suspicious thoughts getting in the way of your social life, you might want to have a goal to go out more. If you find your suspicious thoughts are all you think about, it would probably be good to have a goal to stop being so preoccupied by them.

Typical goals for dealing with suspicious thoughts

Here are some typical goals that people set themselves:

• I want my suspicious thoughts to occur less often.

• I want to be able to cope better with my suspicious thoughts.

• I'd like to reduce the distress they cause me.

• I want to stop believing that my fears might be true.

• I'd like to change the way I react.

• I want to get on with my life and stop these thoughts from interfering all the time.

• I want to stop avoiding social situations.

• I want to be able to relax with people rather than being suspicious of them.

• I need to understand why I have these thoughts and then move on.

- I want to get into the habit of checking whether my fears are true rather than just assuming they are.
- I'd like to get more control over my suspiciousness.
- I want to enjoy my life more.

Write down your goals in your notebook or, if you prefer, in the space provided here:

[Space left intentionally blank in the original book]

Follow the six steps we present over the next three chapters and you will make real progress with your goals.

Step 1: Track your suspicious thoughts week by week

Keeping a record of your suspicious thoughts is the only sure way for you to see how much progress you're making. You may not be very good at recognizing your achievements. Many people focus on what hasn't gone as well as they'd like, and overlook all the good work they've done.

If you regularly track your experience of suspicious thoughts you will also have an accurate picture of how your thinking changes over time. People often forget how frequent and distressing their suspicious thoughts used to be. Your notebook will be a fantastic historical record, showing you just how far you've come, and how much further you want to go. It can also be useful in pinpointing what has helped most: you can see whether a particular exercise or change in behavior has made a difference.

Exercise: Tracking your suspicious thoughts

We suggest you track your suspicious thoughts in the following way.

First, write down the suspicious thought that's worrying you most.

[Space left intentionally blank in the original book]

Now rate:

• How strongly you believe it (give a figure of 0–100 per cent) _____;

• How distressing you find it (give a figure of 0–10 with 0 meaning not distressing and 10 meaning extremely distressing) _____;

• The approximate number of times a day that you think about it _____.

Do this exercise at the end of each week. You can plot your progress by entering your ratings on to the graphs entitled "Graph 1: How strongly you believe the thought., Graph 2: How distressing the thought is., Graph 3: The approximate number of times a day you think about it., Graph 1: How strongly Emily believed the thought."

If you have another suspicious thought that is particularly concerning, you can also rate that and add the scores to the graphs.

The graphs entitled "Graph 2: How distressing the thought was for Emily., Graph 3: The approximate number of times a day Emily thought it." were drawn up by Emily as she monitored her suspicious thoughts over an eight-week period. She tracked the thought:

> *People laugh at me or talk negatively about me behind my back.*

You can see that Emily improved over time, though there was an occasional blip when she felt worse.

Step 2: Increase your understanding of your suspicious thoughts

Step 1 is all about tracking the effect that suspicious thoughts have on you. Step 2 is designed to help you *understand* these experiences.

To help you do this we'd like you to try four exercises. If you stick with them you will increase your awareness of the factors that lead to your suspicious thoughts and you'll have a much clearer idea of why you have these experiences.

You probably will also find that you're able to cope better with your suspicious thoughts. Many people tell us that they notice an improvement simply by doing these exercises. There's a reason for this: doing the exercises actually *changes* the way we experience our suspicious thoughts.

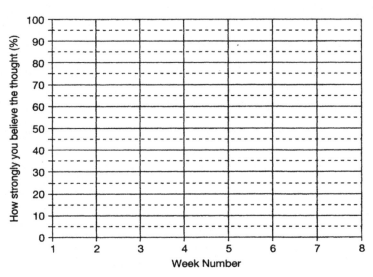

Graph 1: How strongly you believe the thought.

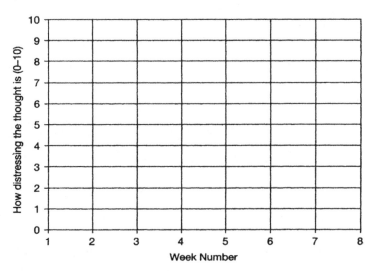

Graph 2: How distressing the thought is.

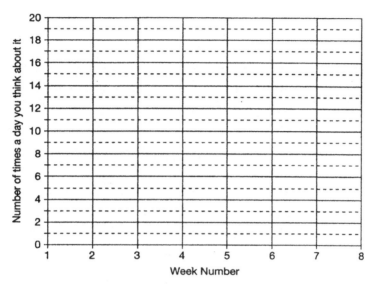

Graph 3: The approximate number of times a day you think about it.

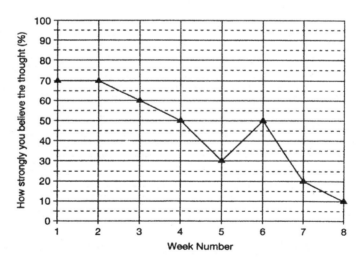

Graph 1: How strongly Emily believed the thought.

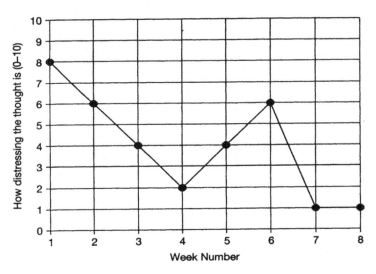

Graph 2: How distressing the thought was for Emily.

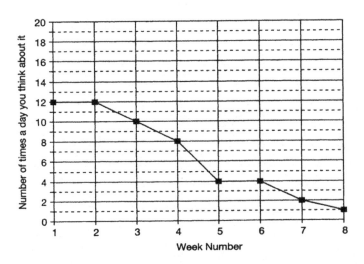

Graph 3: The approximate number of times a day Emily thought it.

Basically, the exercises help us get some *distance* from our thoughts. It won't happen instantly, of course, but gradually you will become much more skilled at detecting your suspicious thoughts as soon as they occur. You won't need to think back over the day to spot them; instead, you'll notice them there and then. And, when you notice them, you will probably also find yourself beginning to think about what's prompted them and how they're affecting you. You will be *analyzing* your thoughts rather than being emotionally caught up in them.

Why does being able to analyze your suspicious thoughts help? Well, as we saw in Chapters 4 and 5, the way you *feel* plays a big role in the occurrence of suspicious thoughts. It's often a circular process: negative emotions like anxiety or depression seem to prompt suspicious thoughts; the suspicious thoughts make you feel anxious or depressed, which then provokes more paranoia.

Taking a step back from your worries disrupts this vicious circle. Instead of getting distressed by your suspicious thoughts, you're concentrating on trying to understand them. And because you're less distressed, the suspicious thoughts have less to feed on. As a result they are easier to manage and less likely to recur.

So there's a double incentive for you to do these exercises. They will help you understand your suspicious thoughts – an essential step in your long-term effort to cope with your fears. But they will also give you a more immediate boost, breaking the cycle of negative emotions that sustains and perpetuates suspicious thoughts.

Exercise A: Keep a diary for a week

It's all too easy to forget the exact form your suspicious thoughts take, when they occur and how they affect you. However, without these details it's hard to really understand what's going on, so we suggest that you keep a diary. Start by doing so for a week. Make sure you fill it in every day when the experience is fresh in your mind. It's best to write up your diary at the same time each day – it will help you make it part of your routine. We've found the following format works well:

Date	Time	What was I doing?	How was I feeling?	What was my suspicious thought?	How did I react?

Here's an extract from Keith's diary:

Date	Time	What was I doing?	How was I feeling?	What was my suspicious thought?	How did I react?
Sunday	3.00 p.m.	At home, watching TV.	Bored, a bit down.	Found myself thinking about work. Worried about the treatment I was going to get from work mates tomorrow. My thought was: 'They all hate me. They're against me.'	Felt quite stressed. Spent the next hour or so worrying.
Sunday	Eve.	Ironing clothes for the week.	Still stressed at the prospect of work.	Thought about the report that my boss has asked me to write. Meeting with him on Wednesday. Am pleased with it but had the thought: 'No matter what I write he's going to pick it to pieces. He has it in for me.' I even thought then: 'He might set the others on to me to rough me up.'	Got angry with my boss! Then was angry with myself for caring.

Date	Time	What was I doing?	How was I feeling?	What was my suspicious thought?	How did I react?
Monday	5.30 a.m.	In bed. Just woken up.	Very tense.	Had a sense that today was going to be hard. Remembered how well I used to get on with everyone and spent a long time thinking about how I got from there to here. Thought: 'This hassle is going to continue. It's psychological warfare.' Carried on worrying all the way to work.	Sad. Anxious about the day ahead.
Monday	9.00 p.m.	At home, reading the paper.	Quite relaxed, but very tired.	Struck me that today had actually been fine at work. Had gone out for a drink with team at lunchtime (Chris's birthday). All very friendly. But boss wasn't there and I thought: 'If my boss was here he'd say something to get at me.'	Cross at boss, cross with myself for having these thoughts even after a good day.

After you've kept your diary for a week, read it through a couple of times and think about these questions:

What triggers my suspicious thoughts?

• Are my suspicious thoughts more likely to occur in particular situations?

• Am I more likely to have these thoughts when I'm busy or when I'm not doing much?

• What kind of a mood am I in just before I have a suspicious thought? Is it different to normal?

• Do I feel different inside just before I have a suspicious thought?

• Do I tend to be expecting trouble or hostility from other people before I have a suspicious thought?

• Are any negative or unhappy images going through my mind in the run-up to a suspicious thought?

How do I react to my suspicious thoughts?

• Do I feel anxious when I have a suspicious thought?

Do I feel more anxious than normal?

> • Do I start to panic when I have these thoughts?
> • Do I try to get away from the situation I'm in?
> • Do I treat the thought as if it's true?
> • Do I try to think through what's happening?
> • What do I do to try to cope with the thought?

Exercise B: Write about your suspicious thoughts

Try writing a description of your experiences with suspicious thoughts. Concentrate on what was happening on one recent occasion and how you felt. Don't try to analyze things. What we want you to put down on paper are the exact details of your experience and it's hard to do that if you are also trying to work out what it all means. Just describing your experiences in this very focused way will help you learn about your fears and the kinds of judgments and assumptions you make while having suspicious thoughts.

One technique that people sometimes find helpful is to imagine that they're writing a movie script. You need to tell the director (or maybe the actor playing you) exactly what's going on, and exactly what you're thinking, at every moment – and in chronological order. Describe the scene in as much detail as you can. Try to capture every twist and turn of your thoughts and feelings. Write down your thoughts, even if they now seem embarrassing. If any images went through your mind, try to describe those as clearly as you can. Remember, what you're trying to get down is *the way it felt from moment to moment* – don't worry about anything else at this point.

Choose a recent occasion when you've had a troubling suspicious thought. When you've finished describing your experience (don't write more than one page), try to do it again for two more episodes. As an example, here's something written by Emily:

A drinks party for Carrie. She was leaving the firm – relocating to New Zealand. There were about thirty of us in the pub. It was Friday night so the place was packed. Everyone was in week-end mode. I had a very nice time chatting to people.

After a while found myself with Carrie, who I like, and Francis (one of the senior partners). Francis is okay but I've always found him a bit intimidating. Anyhow, Carrie, Francis and I were standing there talking and he said he was really sorry to see Carrie go and that working with her had always been a pleasure. He was sure she was going to be a huge success in New Zealand. I found myself trying to remember a single word of praise that Francis had ever given me. We've worked together quite a bit but I couldn't think of anything. I suddenly felt angry and upset. I felt that Francis clearly didn't rate me, just like the other senior partners. I told myself that he was just saying the sort of thing everyone said at a leaving do – in fact, I'd already heard lots of comments like this that evening and none of them had bothered me. I knew I was reacting unreasonably, but that didn't help. I had another of the thoughts I quite often have: everyone thinks I'm rubbish, they want me to leave.

Then Francis (who'd been looking straight at Carrie) glanced at me and I was convinced that this was his way of pointing out to me that his little compliments to Carrie were meant to send a message to me. That did it: I knew I had to get out of there before I burst into tears or said something stupid. I went to the Ladies and hoped that Francis hadn't been able to tell how much he'd got to me. As usual in these situations, I felt ridiculous and ashamed of myself – and really disappointed that an enjoyable evening had ended badly again.

Exercise C: Go looking for a suspicious thought

This exercise is one to try when you're feeling confident.

The exercises we've described so far are all retrospective: they involve looking back at suspicious thoughts after they've occurred. But this one is different and at first it might sound a little strange. We'd like you to try to have a suspicious thought. Think of a situation that's likely to provoke your fears and then put yourself into that situation.

Why on earth would I want to do that, you might well be thinking! Well, it's a fantastic learning opportunity. It's not something to try if you're feeling down or anxious or struggling to cope (if you are, skip to Exercise D). But when things are going better it gives you the perfect chance to observe yourself as you experience a suspicious thought. Because you know the thought is likely to be coming, you can be ready for it. Instead of trying hours later to remember what happened you get a real-time insight into the triggers, the feelings and your reactions. It's your own personal show, a chance to settle into your seat and watch what it's like to have a paranoid thought. When you're doing this, try to be aware of how you feel before going into the situation, the internal and external experiences that are leading you to think suspiciously, and your reaction (your thoughts, feelings and behavior). The information you get from this will help you in the next exercise, which is all about looking at the causes of your suspicious thoughts.

Exercise D: The causes of a suspicious thought

As we've seen, suspicious thoughts don't just arrive out of the blue. Instead, they are the product of a combination of powerful factors. If you can under-

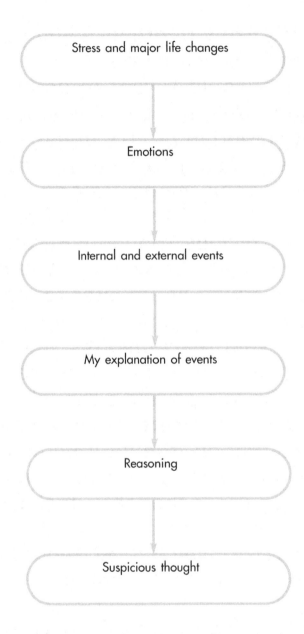

stand how these factors combine you will find it eas-ier to deal with your suspicious thoughts.

Chapters 4 and 5 set out the typical causes of paranoid thoughts. Now we want you to take that theoretical knowledge and use it to understand your own experiences. Look back at the suspicious thoughts you drew on for Exercises A, B and C. Choose the one that affected you most strongly and then fill in the blank diagram below. Try to fill in the diagram without looking back at the previous chapters. When you have finished look back at Chapters 4 and 5 to see whether you've forgotten an important factor.

Stress and major life changes
Just back to work after having Lily; finding it hard to cope with work and childcare. Lack of sleep.

↓

Emotions
Stressed; tired; feeling quite vulnerable and insecure.

↓

Internal and external events
Hot. Anxious inside. Senior partner ignored me, complimented someone else, then glanced at me. Had been drinking too, which probably didn't help.

↓

My explanation of events
As usual I was trying to find the hidden meaning in someone's comments. When Francis looked at me, I knew it was all about my weaknesses and their bad opinion of me.

↓

Reasoning
I tend to think the worst of other people – or at least other people at work. I jump to conclusions & always think I've got it figured out – that I've seen through people.

↓

Suspicious thought
Senior partners think I'm no good at my job and want me out.

Please use the space provided below to make notes before filling in the diagram.

This is the diagram that Emily completed for the experience she described before at her colleague's leaving party:

Once you have completed the two steps we've described in this chapter you will have:

• An up-to-date record of how much you're affected by suspicious thoughts and the way your experience changes over time;

• A greater understanding of how your suspicious thoughts are caused and how you react to them;

• Gained some distance from your paranoid thoughts by learning how to observe and analyze them.

The next two chapters set out the remaining four steps that will help you overcome your suspicious thoughts.

CHAPTER SUMMARY

• There are six practical steps you can take to overcome your suspicious thoughts.

• The first two steps are designed to help you develop a detailed understanding of how and when your suspicious thoughts affect you.

- To gain this understanding you need to become a detached observer of your anxieties.
- You have a much better chance of succeeding with these steps if you can support them with the right kind of attitude and behaviors.

7

Challenging paranoid and suspicious thoughts

Introduction

Suspicious thoughts don't just come out of the blue. They are our attempt to make sense of our experiences.

The world around us, and even the way we feel inside, can sometimes seem quite mysterious. When it comes down to it, it's often very hard to be sure what our experiences really mean. Perhaps because it is so difficult, we tend to interpret the present by looking back to the past. When something happens to us we remember similar experiences that we've had. This is perfectly natural: we use the knowledge we've gained over the course of our lives to help us in the present.

There's a drawback, though. If we're not careful our past experiences can get in the way of us seeing what's really going on in the here and now. We develop *preconceptions* about the world and don't stop to consider how accurate they are.

This can be a particular problem if you're prone to suspicious thoughts. If you've had negative experiences in the past – being bullied, for instance

– you may well worry that other people will behave in the same way towards you in the future. If you're used to seeing other people as a threat it's hard to break out of that mindset.

We need to shake up our preconceptions. Don't let your reactions to your experiences become set in stone: challenge them! Even if your views were right in the past they may not be right now.

This chapter is all about *testing* your preconceptions. We want you to reassess the way you make sense of your experiences. Challenging the way you think is hard. It can be like trying to unlearn a reflex. But you can definitely do it. You will find it easier to do when you're calm – you will not be in the mood to reassess anything if you're feeling really stressed or upset. The knowledge you've gained about how and why your suspicious thoughts occur will be a big help. And so too will the techniques and exercises we set out in this chapter.

The rules of good decision-making

Suspicious thoughts are a normal part of life: everyone has them. After all, we have a lot of ambiguous information to make sense of whether it be, for example, the look on some-one's face, a comment we overhear or perhaps seeing the same car several times behind us on a journey.

It's our *reaction* to these thoughts that makes the difference. We have to decide how seriously to take them. And that decision can be crucial. When we're feeling down or anxious or stressed it's all too easy to jump to conclusions and assume the worst. But we need to treat these kinds of thoughts with real caution. You can help yourself make good decisions about them by following these five rules:

- Don't treat thoughts and feelings as facts.
- Think of the evidence both for and against a thought.
- Always try to think of alternative explanations for an event.
- Test out your explanations.
- Keep an open mind.

Let's look at each of these rules in a little more detail.

Don't treat thoughts and feelings as facts

Scientific research has shown something very important about the way we think and make decisions: we rarely do it logically.

Our thoughts tend to come to us very quickly, so quickly in fact that it feels as if they're happening automatically. They aren't based on what psychologists would call logical reasoning. They aren't the product of careful consideration, rigorous testing and thorough review. Instead, they're usually rooted in guesswork, feelings and intuition.

This is fair enough. After all, we have thousands of thoughts each day, most of which come and go without making much of an impression on us. It's hardly surprising that they're rather more haphazard than they are logical. But it does mean that we shouldn't treat them as if they were facts or truths. Most of our thoughts are just a first snap reaction to what we see or feel.

It's the same with our feelings: we can't rely on them to give us an accurate picture of the world. Just because we *feel* threatened doesn't mean that we are. Making judgments and decisions on the basis of feelings is very risky.

When you have a thought or feeling about something that happens to you, don't assume it's correct. It might be, but it might also be wrong. Or it might be half-right. To find out which it is, we need to apply some logical reasoning – which just happen to be the next four rules of good decision-making.

Think of evidence both for and against a thought

Chapter 5 looked at how once we start to believe a thought is true we notice all the evidence that seems to support it and none that doesn't. This is what psychologists call the *belief confirma-*

tion bias and it explains why, in her lowest moments, Emily would focus only on the parts of her evening out that she saw as proving that her colleagues had a low opinion of her. That might be one overheard comment or one glance in her direction. The rest of the evening, which she might have spent chatting happily with people, meant nothing to her. For Emily, the good things that happened were so insignificant they might as well not have happened at all.

Before you decide that a suspicious thought is true, **weigh the evidence.** You need to consider both the evidence that supports your thought *and* the evidence that doesn't. If Emily sees a senior colleague look across the room at her with what might have been a frown on his face, she has two sets of evidence to consider. On the one hand is her sense that the colleague really was frowning at her and the view held by several people in her firm that he has a low opinion of relatively young women lawyers. This might mean that he's thinking negative thoughts about Emily. This might be typical of the way *all* the senior partners in the firm think about her.

On the other hand, Emily needs to think through the pos sibility that her colleague may not have been looking at her and that, even if he was, he may not actually have been *thinking* about her. He might have been thinking of a thousand and one other things, or he might have been lost in a daydream. In any case, perhaps his eyesight isn't good enough to pick her out in a darkened room. Emily might also remember that she actually worked on a case with this man a year ago and found him perfectly friendly. It's possible then that the gossip in the office about his views on women lawyers is wrong. As for the other senior partners in the firm, Emily has had a friendly working relationship with some, a less positive experience with a couple of others and hasn't worked at all with most of them. It would be hard for her to come to any firm conclusions about how they all view her.

Once you spend a little time thinking through the evidence for a thought, you will generally find that your first reaction to a situation isn't completely correct. You get a much more balanced perspective when you consider both sides of the argument. And with a balanced perspective you're in a much better position to get an accurate understanding of what you've been experiencing.

Always try to think of alternative explanations for an event

As part of your effort to weigh the evidence, you need to consider whether there are *alternative explanations* for the event that's prompted your suspicious thought. There are almost always lots of potential explanations for any event, as the example we've just discussed involving Emily shows. You just have to take the time to think them through.

It's very important that you do consider the options in this way because the explanation you choose has such a big effect on the way you feel. If Emily thinks her colleague is frowning at her, it fuels her sense of being undervalued at work. On the other hand, if she decides he probably wasn't looking at her she's likely to feel a lot better about herself and her colleagues.

Test out your explanations

Let's recap for a moment. The things that happen to us in life prompt all kinds of off-the-cuff thoughts and feelings. Before we set too much store by these first reactions, we need to step back and think them through. Let's try to imagine all the possible explanations and think through the evidence to decide which is most likely to be true.

But we can do more than just think about these possibilities: we can actually *test* them. Psychologists call it *reality testing.* For example, you might not have seen some old friends for several months and be worrying that they're avoiding you for some reason. One possible explanation is that you've accidentally upset them and so they are indeed keeping their distance. Another explanation is that they've been going through some tough times and are keeping themselves to themselves. And a third might be that you've all been really busy with work and other commitments and that your friends would love to see you again. You can test out these explanations in several ways. For example, you could ask a mutual friend for their take on the situation. Or you could invite your friends over for the evening and see how you all get on. You could even admit your worries to them, give them a call and see how they react.

It isn't always easy to think of one single test that will give us convincing proof that a suspicious thought is true or not. But if we try out two or three it will be easier to see which explanation seems most plausible.

Keep an open mind

This rule is perhaps the hardest of all, but also the most important.

Most of us want certainty most of the time. We want to know what's going on around us, and we want to understand it too. It's a way of feeling in control of our lives – and who doesn't want to feel in control?

But whether we like it or not, we all have to accept that there are some things we can't know for sure. Sometimes we just have to be comfortable with uncertainty.

This is especially important when you're dealing with suspicious thoughts. If an event or experience has been bothering you, think through the possible explanations and decide which, on the balance of the evidence, seems most likely to be true. But don't go chasing a certainty you may never achieve. Say, for example, a stranger on a bus stares at you in an unfriendly way. You might feel sure he was being hostile but there's no way of knowing for certain what he was really thinking. A little doubt is a healthy thing – it's a sign that we're keeping our minds open rather than jumping to conclusions.

Now let's apply these five rules of good decision-making in Steps 3 and 4 to overcoming suspicious thoughts.

Step 3: Review the evidence

In Step 3 we want you to try three exercises designed to help you think through the evidence for your suspicious thoughts.

Exercise A: Assess the evidence for your main suspicious thought

First, write down the suspicious thought that's worrying you most.

[Space left intentionally blank in the original book]

Next rate how strongly you believe it (give a figure of 0–100 per cent). _____

Now use the table below to list the evidence that supports the thought – and the evidence that doesn't.

Evidence for:	Evidence against:

It's often difficult to think of the evidence against our suspicious thoughts, especially if those thoughts are causing us distress. If you're finding it hard, ask yourself these questions:

- Is there anything that might suggest the thought could be wrong?
- What would my family or friends say if I talked to them about the thought? (It would actually be a great idea to ask them.)
- What would I say to a friend who came to me with a similar problem?
- What good things have happened to me that contradict the thought?
- Are there any alternative explanations for what seems to have happened?
- Are my thoughts based more on the way I feel than on solid evidence?
- Have I been jumping to conclusions?
- Am I exaggerating the chances of anything bad happening to me?
- Am I being over-sensitive?
- Am I misinterpreting things because I'm feeling anxious or down?
- If I were feeling happier would I still think of things in the same way?
- Are my past experiences getting in the way of me seeing the present situation clearly?

After you've filled in the table spend some time thinking about what you've written and then once more rate how strongly you believe the thought (0–100 per cent).

Exercise B: Assessing your suspicious thoughts over the course of a week

In Chapter 6 we asked you to keep a diary of your suspicious thoughts. You can use that diary to help you complete this exercise. We want you to keep a record of your suspicious thoughts over the course of the week. Then, in much the same way as you did in the previous exercise, review the evidence for and against each of your thoughts. It's best to do this at a set time every day – that way it becomes a habit. In the column marked 'Rating', give a score of 0–100 per cent for how strongly you believe the thought after considering all the evidence for it.

Date	Suspicious thought	How strongly you believed it at the time (0–100%)	Evidence for	Evidence against	Rating after considering evidence (0–100%)

Date	Suspicious thought	How strongly you believed it at the time (0–100%)	Evidence for	Evidence against	Rating after considering evidence (0–100%)
Sunday	They all hate me. They're against me.	90%	1. They look at me oddly. 2. I can see hate in their eyes. 3. They rarely come up and chat to me now. 4. On Friday I heard laughter when I left the room.	1. It's hard to be sure what people's expressions mean or the thoughts in their heads- actually, my face probably doesn't look too friendly a lot of the time. 2. People have gone to lunch with me and do sometimes ask me to the pub. 3. Most of the time nothing bad actually happens. 4. They could have been laughing at anything when I left the room. 5. Some of the lads are actually quite friendly towards me and always say hello.	20%

Here's an example from Keith's diary:

Exercise C: Assessing the alternative explanation

We've seen that suspicious thoughts are caused by a combination of factors. In the last chapter we asked you to fill in a diagram showing how your own suspicious thoughts are produced. Have a look at that diagram now.

You will probably find that there's a lot of information in your diagram. It's probably not the simplest explanation you've ever come across! This isn't surprising – paranoia is a complex thing to explain. Because of this, it's often helpful to think of a phrase or two that sums up the key points you see in the diagram. Here are some examples:

- I'm a worrier.
- I'm always jumping to conclusions.
- The experiences I've had in the past have made me a bit over-sensitive.
- I dwell on things more than I should.
- I tend to get very stressed.
- My imagination runs away with me sometimes.
- I seem to always assume the worst in any situation.
- I'm not good at thinking of alternative explanations for stuff that happens.
- I read too much into people's expressions.

• I often feel vulnerable, but I know they're only feelings.

When you look at the diagram you completed, what phrase comes to mind? Write it down now.

[Space left intentionally blank in the original book]

Have a look back at the diagram Emily produced above. She was assessing her reaction to events at her colleague's leaving party. Emily summarized her diagram with the comments:

- *The way I react is pretty much determined by how stressed I am.*
- *I use any little thing to prove that my own sense of insecurity is justified.*

Emily's initial feeling had been that her suspicious thought had been caused by her colleague's behavior – it was as simple as that. But these comments tell a different story. As the diagram shows, there's much more at work than first meets the eye.

Your diagram will probably also offer you a different story, an alternative explanation for your suspicious thoughts. Using the same scale as before (0–100 per cent), rate how strongly you believe this account. Now we're going to apply the same sort of careful assessment to this alternative explanation as we did in the earlier exercises to the suspicious thoughts. Using the table below, jot down the evidence that supports the explanation and the evidence that doesn't. Take as much time as you need – try to really think through all of the possibilities.

Evidence for:	Evidence against:

Once you've filled in the table read it through and then reassess how strongly you believe it. Write down your new rating. _____

When you look back at your alternative explanation do you find it convincing? We hope that it provides a better account of your experiences than the suspicious thought. If it doesn't you might need to make a few changes: have a look back at Chapters 4 and 5 to help you do this. Don't think of your alternative explanation as set in stone. As you think more about your experiences, and as new things happen in your life, revisit this alternative account and make the changes you think are right.

Step 4: Test your suspicious thoughts

Step 3 gives you the chance to see how likely it is that your suspicious thoughts have been correct. If the evidence seems to back them up then you really may have been in danger. On the other hand, you may well find that there's plenty of evidence to suggest that you've come to the wrong conclusion about what's going on.

Assessing the evidence for your thoughts like this is very useful, but it's *retrospective.* So instead of thinking back to things that have happened in the past, we want you to test out your suspicions on *new experiences.* Don't avoid the situations that trigger your paranoia – go looking for them and see whether your suspicion is actually warranted.

Testing out your fears like this can be a nerve-wracking experience. Don't try it until you've completed the previous three steps and until you're sure that you are ready. It also means you'll have to drop your safety behaviors – the things we do to make it less likely that the thing we fear will actually happen. (If you want to refresh your memory on safety behaviors, have a look back at Chapters 3 and 5.) Testing your fears will involve putting yourself in situations that your safety behaviors would normally help you avoid.

Safety behaviors may appear to be saving us from harm, but they actually just keep our suspicious thoughts going. It can seem as if the safety behaviors are the reason that nothing bad has happened to us when actually it's because we're not actually in danger.

Abandoning our safety behaviors isn't easy. It can seem as if we're dropping our guard and that disaster is bound to follow. If you feel this way, here are three tips to help you make the change:

• Take it slowly. Don't just give up all your safety behaviors in one go: do it gradually. Start by dropping the one you feel most comfortable losing and take it step by step from there.

• Think back to a time in your life when you managed quite happily without safety behaviors. Take heart from the fact that you coped in the past and have confidence that you'll be able to do so again in the future.

• Remind yourself of the real benefits you'll get from testing your fears. This isn't to say it won't be hard – it will be. But you have so much to gain. You will discover whether or not the paranoid thoughts that you've been struggling to deal with are justified. That discovery could make a big difference to your life.

DEVISING YOUR TESTS

If you're finding it hard to think of a good test for your suspicious thoughts, try to identify what it is that your thoughts are stopping you from doing. In Emily's case her anxieties made her stay away from social events, especially if they involved colleagues from work. She was sure that people didn't want to talk to her so she was reluctant to join in a conversation. She thought people would just ignore her. For Emily, parties were places where people talked about her, or laughed at her, and all behind her back. A glance in her direction meant a conversation about her; an overheard laugh meant a joke at her expense. She felt completely isolated. She was convinced she was being singled out and that no one else was being treated in the same way.

Emily tested her fears in four ways. Before she carried out each test she predicted what would happen. She then rated her prediction as 0–100 per cent depending on how confident she was that it would prove to be correct. Here are Emily's four tests, her predictions and the results:

1   She would ask two friends whether they often noticed people glancing or staring at them.
    Prediction: Emily was 70 per cent sure that her friends wouldn't have experienced this.
    Result: One friend said they'd been stared at lots of times and the other said it had occasionally happened.

2   She would ask a trusted work colleague whether others minded her being at work social events.
    Prediction: She was 60 per cent certain that her colleague would say that people had been making negative comments about her.
    Result: Emily's colleague was surprised by the question and said that people would like to see more of her. Emily had wondered whether her colleague would be totally honest,

but she could see how genuinely surprised her colleague was and found this very reassuring.

3 She would attend a work social event, join a group of people and try to be sociable.

Prediction: Emily was 85 per cent sure that people wouldn't be friendly towards her and would soon move away.

Result: Some of the evening was difficult and Emily found it hard to join in at first, but she ended up in an interesting – and enjoyable – conversation. People were clearly friendly, greeting her warmly, smiling, asking how she and her family were, and Emily felt more comfortable as the evening went on.

4 She would invite colleagues out for the evening.

Prediction: She was 100 per cent certain that no one would want to come to an event she'd arranged.

Result: Emily really had to pluck up her courage to do this and was very anxious about arranging the event. She started by mentioning the idea to the colleague she'd talked to in the first test. This helped her to ask all her other colleagues to a meal out. Most of the colleagues she invited attended and afterwards one or two people even spontaneously said they should do it again soon.

Testing out your fears is a daunting task. It takes a lot of courage to put yourself in a situation where you will feel at risk. So it's important to

	Situation/activity	Suspicious thought
1		
2		
3		
4		

build up your confidence by starting with the relatively easy tests. You can then work your way up to the tests you find most difficult. This is what psychologists call a *hierarchy of tests.* It's a good idea, by the way, to repeat your tests. That way, you're less likely to see a positive outcome as a lucky fluke. The more you do the tests, the more confidence you will have in the results.

Emily began with tests that involved gathering information by talking to other people. She moved on to doing things she would normally avoid – going out with work colleagues. Finally, she tackled the test she was most dreading and the one she was most certain would end in disaster: organizing a social event with colleagues.

When you're devising a set of tests start by writing down a list of situations or activities you find difficult (for example, attending social events or walking home alone). Now arrange the list in order of difficulty (with the most difficult activity at the bottom). Write down the suspicious thought that is triggered by or related to the situation or activity.

Here is Emily's list:

	Situation/activity	Suspicious thought
1	Share my experiences with friends.	My suspicions will be confirmed: no one else has these kinds of things happen to them at work. Friends will think I'm mad.
2	Ask someone at work about how other people see me.	People think I'm no good at my job. I'm not popular.
3	Try to socialize at work party.	People don't want to spend time with me and try to avoid me as much as possible. The senior staff definitely won't talk to me for long as they want me out.
4	Organize evening out.	People want me out of the company so they're hardly going to want to socialize with me.

Incidentally, don't put yourself in situations where you're likely to be at real risk. You may be worried about going out alone, but we don't recommend you test this by going into a dangerous neighbourhood at night. Concentrate instead on activities that most people would find reasonable and where you think your suspicious thoughts are probably exaggerated.

Aim for four or five tests. As you set about tackling them keep a record of how you get on.

Make sure you note down the following details for each test:

Suspicious thought to be tested	
How strongly do I believe it (0–100%)	
Test	
My prediction	
How sure am I of my prediction (0–100%)	
Result of the test	
My conclusions	
How strongly do I believe the suspicious thought now (0–100%)	

Testing your fears can be tough and it doesn't always go smoothly for everyone. It can really raise anxiety levels at first – the trick is to hang on in there and let the anxiety come down over half an hour or so. Sometimes a test can just be too difficult. If that happens to you go back to doing a test you find less stressful. Don't give up on testing completely though. In our experience people find it extremely helpful. After all, there's no better way to see how closely your suspicious thoughts match up to reality. You may well discover that they don't match up at all. And when that happens you'll find that all kinds of activities you've been shying away from are suddenly open to you again.

CHAPTER SUMMARY

• This chapter covers Steps 3 and 4 of the six practical steps that will help you overcome your suspicious thoughts.

• Suspicious thoughts are our interpretations of the things that happen to us.

• We need to challenge those interpretations rather than just accepting them.

• We can challenge our suspicious thoughts by:

– Assessing the evidence both for and against them

– Testing out our fears.

8

Coping with paranoid and suspicious thoughts as they happen

Introduction

One of the key from this book is one that may seem a bit deflating: *suspicious thoughts are a part of life.* We all have them at some time or other, and it's likely that we always will.

We can't help you avoid suspicious and paranoid thoughts for the rest of your life because it's simply not possible. What we can help you to do though, is learn to cope with them – to manage them in such a way that they don't distress you and they don't affect your day-to-day life.

The practical steps set out in Chapters 6 and 7 will take you a long way toward this goal. Steps 1 and 2 are all about making sure you really understand your suspicious thoughts – and so don't need to fear them. Steps 3 and 4 are designed to help you test out those thoughts and to see just how accurate they really are. If you've tried these first four steps you are probably aware that your suspicions are exaggerated. You're not really in the kind of danger you've been afraid of.

Steps 1 to 4 will certainly help you deal with your suspicious thoughts. But what about the moment when the thought first occurs to you? If you're like most people paranoid thoughts happen when you're in a stressful situation. So it's not surprising if, when the thought occurs, all the knowledge you may have built up about what's causing your suspicious thoughts and how to deal with them goes right out of your head. Later, when you're feeling calm, you're able to remind yourself that your fears have always proved to be wrong. But it's another matter in the heat of the moment.

Steps 5 and 6 will help you deal with your suspicious thoughts as they happen. We'll show you some techniques and strategies to use when you get the thought, and we'll also help you cope with the worry that paranoid fears so often cause.

Step 5: Dealing with your suspicious thoughts as they happen

Coping with suspicious thoughts really boils down to being in the right state of mind. Now you're probably wondering 'How on earth do I do that?' After all, it's hard to keep a positive attitude when you're dealing with what can be very upsetting thoughts.

However, you can *learn* how to get yourself into this state of mind. Step 5 presents four techniques to help you do just that. We can't promise an overnight transformation. If suspicious thoughts have been causing you problems changing the way you react to them isn't going to be easy. But stick with it: given time and practice, these techniques really will make a difference.

1 DON'T FIGHT THE SUSPICIOUS THOUGHT

White elephants.

For the next 60 seconds we want you to *avoid thinking about white elephants.* Keep your mind completely free of them – and if a white elephant seems to be creeping in, suppress the thought as quickly as you can. Probably white elephants aren't something you normally give a lot of thought to so this should be easy, right? Off you go.

We're willing to bet that thoughts of white elephants kept on occurring no matter how hard you tried to put them out of your mind – that's certainly what happened when we tried this exercise. This isn't surprising: lots of research has shown that trying *not* to think about something only makes us think about it more.

When you get a suspicious thought, don't fight it. Don't try to pretend it hasn't happened. Don't try to force it out of your mind. It will only come back, just like those white elephants.

There's another reason why you shouldn't try to suppress a suspicious thought: you don't need to. It isn't giving you news you'd rather forget; it isn't a fact. It's just one of the thousands of thoughts you have each day and you should treat it just like you do any of the others.

2 LET GO OF THE SUSPICIOUS THOUGHT

When a suspicious thought occurs don't try to pretend it hasn't happened. Notice it – and then let it go.

Don't spend time thinking about the thought. Don't bother trying to understand it and definitely don't act on it. Try to be detached, as if you're watching something happen to someone else long ago. Watch the thought come to you, remind yourself that it doesn't matter and let it fade into the distance.

For some people the suspicious thoughts can come in waves, one after the other. If this happens to you don't let those waves drag you down: try to ride them out. Don't let the thoughts upset you and don't try to make them stop coming. We know this is hard, but aim to stay as calm as you can. Hang on in there and watch the waves of thoughts fade into the distance.

You will notice here there's a change of focus in our approach. Steps 1 to 4 were all about analyzing and understanding your suspicious thoughts. If this has gone well you will have realized that your thoughts are probably exaggerated. Now it's time to shift gears and let the thoughts go without all that analysis.

3 GIVE YOURSELF PLENTY OF ADVICE AND ENCOURAGEMENT

People often find it helpful to have a phrase or two they can repeat to themselves when they're experiencing suspicious thoughts. Obviously, that phrase should be a positive one! Think of the advice and encouragement you'd offer a friend who was having these thoughts and then offer it to yourself. Tell yourself you're doing well and that you're going to see off these thoughts. Or remind yourself of the key lessons you've learned from reading this book.

Here are some phrases we've seen used with good results:

- I'm just being over-sensitive.
- They're only thoughts – they don't matter.
- Keep going – you're doing really well.
- I'm jumping to conclusions again. There's no way I can know what she's thinking.
- It's just another of those thoughts – it will pass.

- These thoughts don't scare me. I can cope.

It can be hard to remember all this in the middle of a paranoid thought so you might want to write down your key phrases on a card or piece of paper. Keep it with you and it will always be there when you need it.

Write down a phrase you think will help you deal with your suspicious thoughts.

4 FOCUS ON WHAT YOU'RE DOING, NOT WHAT YOU'RE THINKING

Suspicious thoughts occur in all kinds of situations. You might be at a party, at the cinema, or in a meeting at work. Wherever you happen to be, you can get lost in your thoughts, completely forgetting whatever it is you're doing.

It's important to try not get absorbed in our worries like this: all it does is increase their grip on us. Focus on the task in hand – your conversation with friends at the party, for example, or the film you're watching. Don't let your paranoid thoughts fool you into believing that they are the most important thing going on. Immerse yourself instead in what you're doing, rather than what you're thinking.

Of course suspicious thoughts also come to us when we're not doing anything very much. In fact, for many people they are *more likely* to occur when they don't have anything else to hold their attention. When we look back at the extract from Keith's diary in Chapter 6, we can see that it's really *only* when he's not doing a lot that his paranoid thoughts surface: watching TV, reading the paper, lying in bed, ironing. All of these situations are ones in which it's easy for the mind to wander and most people's minds tend to wander back to their preoccupations. If you're not doing much when you have a suspicious thought try to put the thought to one side and get on with doing something you really enjoy.

Like many of the other techniques we set out in this book, these four strategies need practice and preparation. Think of a typical situation in which you experience suspicious thoughts. How would you like yourself to react if a paranoid thought occurs? Visualize the thought occurring and your response to it. Don't worry about how you're actually likely to react, or how you've reacted in the past. Concentrate instead on your *ideal* reaction.

When you have visualized the scene it's a good idea to write it down – it will be a useful reminder of how you'd like to react in the future. Here's the note Keith wrote:

Sat at home watching TV on Sunday afternoon. Daydreaming. Started worrying about work. We always have team meetings on a Monday morning. Feel like these are turning into a chance for the boss to pick on me. Usually these thoughts prey on me. I can spend hours (or at least what feels like hours) turning them over in my mind. This time, though, I didn't let it get to me. I just told myself that it's what I always end up thinking on a Sunday afternoon, that it doesn't matter and that I can't be bothered spending more energy on it. Said to myself a few times: 'It's just the usual nonsense. It'll be gone in a minute or so.' Then I got up off the sofa and went and rang my eldest to fix up a time for when I could go and visit her.

You can see in Keith's description how he doesn't try to pretend that the thought hasn't happened. Instead of fighting it he stays calm and manages to get some distance from the experience. In fact, it's almost as if he were watching it happen to someone else. He gives himself some words of encouragement and advice and then makes sure he focuses on something that really absorbs him – planning to see his daughter.

Try writing your own account of how you would ideally react to your suspicious thoughts.

Step 6: Dealing with worry

Look back again at Keith's diary in section entitled "Here's an example from Keith's diary". You can see that he usually responds to his suspicious thoughts by worrying. In fact, he spends a lot of time worrying – sometimes hours at a stretch. He worries about how his colleagues will treat him. He worries that his manager is going to criticize his work. Sometimes he just seems to worry about the day ahead – nothing specific, just a sense that something bad may happen.

That's what worry is: an anxiety that something bad will happen and wondering what will happen to us if it does.

Keith isn't unusual: worry is a common reaction to suspicious thoughts. For some people, worry can seem a way of preventing harm: it's like keeping a lookout for danger.

But what's wrong with worrying? Shouldn't we be alert to possible trouble? Doesn't it actually make sense to be aware of consequences if something bad does happen?

Well, let's see what worry can *really* do for us.

LEARNING ABOUT WORRY

When we worry we think about the consequences of something bad happening. What if my boss thinks my work isn't up to scratch? What if I've done something to offend my friends? What if I miss my train?

Let's play the 'What if' game with a trivial negative event – in this case, accidentally spilling some food on our clothes at lunch.

What bad thing might happen if you spill your food?

Write it down.

- Then what bad thing might happen? Write it down.
- Then what bad thing might happen? Write it down.
- Then what bad thing might happen? Write it down.
- Then what bad thing might happen? Write it down.

Here's what we came up with when we did this exercise:

What bad thing might happen if you spill your food? *It will make a mark on my shirt.*

- Then what bad thing might happen? *I'd look messy and unprofessional.*
- Then what bad thing might happen? *My boss might notice.*
- Then what bad thing might happen? *She'd think badly of me.*
- Then what bad thing might happen? *It might influence the way she feels about me – and my contract is due for renewal soon.*
- Then what bad thing might happen? I might not get my contract renewed. I'd be out of work.

So being a bit clumsy at lunchtime has cost us our job! This is pretty far-fetched, of course, but actually that's the way worry works. We spend a lot of time worrying about things that are very unlikely to happen. We don't take a balanced view of the situation; instead *we focus on the negative.* How often do we spend ages worrying about something and then decide that everything is bound to work out okay? Not very often! And the more we worry, the worse we expect things to turn out: *worry feeds on worry.*

For many people, worrying is so much a part of their make-up that the thought of stopping is scary. Worrying feels like a way of *coping,* a way of thinking through and being pre pared for trouble. In reality, it's usually no help at all. We need to stop worrying and start thinking positively. This doesn't mean ignoring life's problems – how could we even if we tried?

But we need to change the way we react to those problems. We need to *manage our worry.* Here are two exercises to help you deal with worry.

Exercise A: Use worry periods

Here's what Keith told us about the effect suspicious thoughts had on him:

> *You asked me how much time I used to spend worrying. Well, basically it took up all of my spare time. At least that's the way it felt when I was at my lowest. If I wasn't totally preoccupied with whatever I was doing, I'd find my worries creeping in again. Then it was more or less impossible to think about anything else. It felt a bit like an addiction. I couldn't give it up, even though I was desperate.*

When we're worried about something getting that anxiety out of our minds for even a short time can seem the hardest thing in the world. As Keith says, worry can be so powerful and uncontrollable that it feels like an addiction.

But just like an addiction worry can be beaten. We asked Keith to save up his worrying for a daily 30-minute 'worry period'. If he found himself worrying at any other time he had to try to postpone his worry till later. Keith's task was to notice when he started to worry but, instead of thinking about it, he had to write it down and save it for his worry period. We suggested that he did his worrying at the same time every day and Keith chose

6.30–7.00p.m., just after he'd got home from work. (Try to avoid making your worry period too close to bed time – if it's the last thing you think about at night you might find it hard to get to sleep.)

It took a bit of time to get the hang of it, but after a few days I got pretty good at postponing my worrying. I said to myself, 'Not now. I'll deal with you later.' In the beginning I'd write down the worry in my notebook so I didn't forget it. I don't need to do that now.

When I got back from work, I'd make myself a cup of tea, sit in my armchair and set my alarm clock for 30 minutes' time. I actually used to look forward to my worrying time – it sounds strange but it was nice feeling that it was okay to worry for that half hour. I didn't feel guilty or embarrassed like I usually did when I worried. In the early weeks I had no problem filling the half hour. It could be a struggle to stop worrying when the alarm went. After a while, though, I either ran out of energy with time left or didn't start at all. I told myself I'd do the worry period tomorrow but when tomorrow came I sometimes didn't do it then either. Maybe I was weaning myself off worrying.

Try using worry periods yourself. You may well find that, like Keith, you stop needing them. Worrying can come to seem much less important to us. And even if that doesn't happen for you, worry periods will help you get on with your life without the constant nagging distraction of your anxieties.

Exercise B: Focus on problem-solving rather than worrying

When we worry we give ourselves a skewed perspective on the world. We focus on the bad things – all the terrible experiences that might happen to us if things go wrong.

This exercise is all about correcting that one-eyed view. In stead of spending all our time dwelling on the negative we need to open up to the positive and constructive things we can do to make our lives better. In particular, let's start to see our suspicious thoughts, and the worries they trigger, as *problems we can solve.*

Begin with the worry periods we describe in Exercise A. Then, when you're ready, aim to replace these worry periods with problem-solving periods.

Focus on the events that normally spark your paranoia. For example, it might be when you think people are getting at you or being too intrusive, or when you're feeling really tired or stressed. What you need to do is change the way you respond to these triggers. Instead of worrying about them, think about how you could deal with these experiences differently.

Problem-solving is all about taking a logical approach to dealing with issues. And because it's logical there's no mystery: we can learn how to do it. Follow the steps we set out below (make sure you write down your answers).

1 Define the problem as specifically as you can.
2 Think of as many solutions to the problem as you possibly can. Try to remember what's worked for you in the past. If you think it might be useful, ask someone you trust for advice. What would you tell someone who came to you with the same problem?
3 Weigh up the pros and cons of each of the possible solutions.
4 Choose the solution you think is best and decide how you're going to carry it out. Try to anticipate the problems you might face with it and think through how you might deal with them.
5 Try out the solution you've chosen. Afterwards, have a think about how well it's worked. If things haven't gone as well as you'd have liked, start the problem-solving process again.

Here's what happened when Keith tried problem-solving:

The problem

The problem is when my boss makes a remark about me or my work in front of other people. I assume he's getting at me.

The solution

I can think of four possible solutions:
1 *Challenge him in the meeting.*

2 *Have a word with him in private and explain the way his behavior makes me feel.*

3 *Ask the other people at work whether they think he's getting at me.*

4 *Try not to react in my normal way. I'd like to able to tell myself it's nothing and that I'm just imagining things as usual. I'd like these sorts of incident to seem really trivial to me. Actually, I'd like to reach the stage where I'm not bothered even if he really is having a go at me.*

Weighing up the pros and cons

Challenging him in the meeting shows I'm not scared of him. It puts me in the driving seat for once. It'll show everyone that I can look after myself. On the other hand, I might make a complete idiot of myself in front of the whole team. I'll probably be so nervous I won't be able to say what I want to say to him. And what if I'm wrong about what he's doing? That's going to be even more embarrassing.

Having a word with him in private feels like a much more sensible idea. We can have an honest, man-to-man conversation. Clear the air and all that. But I'm worried about saying too much or saying the wrong thing. I don't trust myself to stay calm in that situation. And I don't think he'll be very interested in the way I feel. He's not exactly the touchy-feely type.

If I speak to the guys at work I'll get a different perspective on all this. I feel like I'm far too close to it to really know for sure what's happening. If they tell me they don't think he's putting me down, I'll know that I'm just overreacting. If they reckon he is, then I'll know I'm not imagining it all. I'll know I'm not crazy. The only drawback I can see is that they might think I really am mad! And I don't honestly know whether I've got the nerve to talk to other people about this stuff: it feels too personal.

If I try to deal with it on my own I don't get other people's perspective. It just stays as my problem, which is a bit lonely. But at least I don't have to worry about other people's reactions. I don't have to summon up the courage to talk to anyone else. I'll be sorting it out for myself, which will feel good. Also, this is something I've been trying out lately and things have gone quite well.

Choose the solution

I've decided to go with option four. The next time my boss does something to wind me up I'll try to just let it go. I might make a note of a couple of phrases I can use – just in case I get upset or flustered and forget what I'm trying to do. If I do write something down, I don't want the person sitting next to me to see it.

Trying out the solution

At our next team meeting I felt there were a couple of moments when my boss might have been having a dig at me and later in the same meeting I thought he might have been ignoring me. I tried really hard not to let these things get to me. I wrote in my notebook, 'it doesn't matter'. I looked at that and repeated it in my head, over and over. Then I tried to concentrate on remembering all the things Carrie (that's my daughter) and I had done together the other weekend. I might have been in that meeting room physically, but I did my best to be somewhere else in my mind. It worked pretty well – better than I'd expected. I suppose it might have looked as if I was daydreaming, but I won't have been the only one!

Many people find this problem-solving approach helps reduce the number of suspicious thoughts they have. That usually means reducing their anxiety and worry too. And if that isn't a recommendation to give problem-solving a try, we don't know what is!

Staying well

If you've tried all six of the steps we've described in the past three chapters you will doubtless be relieved to know that we don't have any more up our sleeve! The exercises can be very hard work, for sure. But, all being well, they will have been worth the effort.

There's one more task we'd like you to try in order to master suspicious thoughts. No matter how hard we work at dealing with these thoughts we can't hope to get rid of them completely. At some point you're bound to have those feelings again and you might find it hard to cope. It's usually easier to deal with problems if you've prepared a plan in advance – and that's what we want you to write now. Have a think about what you'd do if you were finding it hard to cope with paranoid thoughts in the future. Psychologists give this the not very optimistic name of a *relapse plan;* we prefer to call it an *action plan.*

To help you put together your own action plan, write down:

• The sorts of stresses and problems that are likely to trigger your suspicious thoughts.
• The early warning signs that these thoughts are getting to you (maybe you're drinking more, or feeling less like socializing).
• The steps you'll take to deal with your suspicious thoughts.

Make sure you keep this action plan somewhere safe and somewhere you can easily find it in case you need it in the future.

Here's the action plan Keith came up with:

Triggers: *Things that make me feel alone – for instance, the anniversary of my parents' deaths. Or if something happens at work – maybe someone new starting who isn't very friendly or if colleagues are laughing at a joke I don't get. I need to be careful with these sorts of things.*

Warning signs: *Worrying is always the biggest sign for me and wanting to spend less time with other people. Also feeling unsettled* *and stressed. If I'm not sleeping, that's usually a sign that things are getting worse.*

What I'll do: *I'll definitely look at the book again for ideas. Star ting worry periods again will help. Will also plan some good things (maybe catching up with the kids). And I'll try to talk to someone about my worries. The trick is going to be to catch things early, imp rove my mood and not get caught up in my suspicious thoughts.*

We hope the six practical steps we've shown you over the course of Chapters 6, 7 and 8 have been a real help in your efforts to deal with your suspicious thoughts. But there's more you can do to really get on top of these thoughts. It's quite simple: keep yourself happy and healthy. In Chapter 9 we'll show you how.

CHAPTER SUMMARY

• Coping with suspicious thoughts is all about being in the right state of mind.

• When a suspicious thought comes to you, try to:

– avoid fighting the thought or pretending it hasn't happened;

– let it go – be as calm and detached as you can;

– remind yourself what you're trying to achieve and give yourself plenty of encouragement;

– focus on what you're doing and not what you're thinking.

- We need to learn to deal with the worry that suspicious thoughts so often cause. To do this save up all your worrying for one half hour session every day: your **worry period.**

- Instead of worrying, try solving the problem that prompts you to worry in the first place **(problem-solving).**

- Make sure you write down an **action plan** to help you deal with suspicious thoughts if they get out of hand again in the future.

9

Feeling good about yourself

Introduction

How many suspicious thoughts do you have when you're feeling really happy and healthy? And if you do have them when you're feeling very happy, how badly do they affect you?

The world looks different when we're happy and well. In fact, it doesn't just look different: it looks *better.* In this frame of mind we're much less likely to be suspicious of other people and if we do have suspicious thoughts, the chances are we'll just ignore them.

However, when we're feeling down or upset or anxious, we're much more likely to have problems with paranoid thoughts. Take a look back at Chapters 4 and 5 and you'll see the large part that negative emotions play in causing and sustaining troubling suspicious thoughts.

If you can improve the way you feel about yourself and the world (your mood), you'll reduce the number of paranoid thoughts you have. And because problems are so much easier to deal with when you're feeling positive, you'll be in a much better position to cope with those thoughts if they do occur. This chapter is all about improving your mood by building a happy and healthy lifestyle.

What causes our moods?

In order to improve our mood we first need to understand how those moods are *caused.*

Throughout this book we draw on the pioneering psychological research of cognitive therapy. Cognitive therapy was originally developed to help people deal with low mood – by which we mean feeling down or depressed or sad or anxious or worried. The American psychiatrist Dr Aaron Beck is one of the founders of cognitive therapy and his work has given us important insights into the causes of low mood. Basically, our moods are the product of:

- Our thoughts;
- The way we make sense of the world;
- Our behavior.

Let's look at each of these three factors in a bit more detail.

Our thoughts

You might think that it's what happens to us in our lives that has the biggest influence on how we feel. We can capture this in a simple diagram:

Events ➜ ➜ ➜ Feelings

After all, if we're going through a rough patch in a relationship or have lost our job, for instance, we're naturally going to feel down, aren't we?

Well, not necessarily. More often than not, it's actually the way we *think about* those events that determines how we're going to feel. Take, for instance, a group of people who've all been made redundant by the same employer. Their reactions to this apparently negative event may be very different. One person might think: 'Fantastic. I should have made a move by now anyway. This is the kick up the backside I need to get on and do what I really want to with my career.' This person probably feels happy. Another might take a philosophical view of events: 'It's a shame, but these things happen. I knew the company was struggling so I wasn't surprised. I'll find something else and I've got the redundancy package to help me until I do.' For someone else being laid off is much more traumatic: 'I knew they wanted to get rid of me. This is just the excuse they've been waiting for. It's how they always get shot of people they don't rate. What on earth am I going to do now?' This per son probably feels miserable.

We can't predict how someone is going to feel just by looking at what's happened to them. To know how they feel, we have to know *what they're thinking.* A change is needed to our diagram:

Events ➜ ➜ ➜ Thoughts ➜ ➜ ➜ Feelings

Events cause us to think certain thoughts that in turn produce particular feelings. And *negative thoughts produce negative feelings:they make us unhappy.* On the other hand, *thinking positively will help us feel happier.*

The way we make sense of the world

Thinking is the way we make sense of the world and our experiences. It's hugely influenced by our mood, but it also then *reinforces* our mood as we'll see below. When we're feeling down the way we think may well be affected in one or more of the following ways:

• **All or nothing thinking:** Things can look very black and white when we're not feeling great. Life is either great or terrible; we're either a total success or a complete failure. If we're feeling down we'll probably see life as terrible and ourselves as a failure. We don't tend to be very interested in a more balanced view of the situation: it's all or nothing.

• **Ignoring the positive:** It's hard to see the good things when our mood is low. We focus on all the bad stuff and anything else is either invisible to us or insignificant. For example, if someone praises us for a piece of work we've done, we'll probably decide that they're just being polite or that they've not noticed the problems in our work. It's the belief confirmation bias all over again (in section entitled "Believing that our suspicions may be true" for more on this). In fact, research has shown that our mood affects our *memory:* when we're down, we actually find it much easier to remember negative experiences than we do positive ones.

• **Taking things personally:** When we're feeling low it can seem as if every little event is a result of something we've done. If someone moves away from us

on the bus, it's because they don't like the way we look and not because they want to have a seat to themselves. If our boss is grumpy in a Mon day morning meeting, it's because we've done something to annoy them and not because she slept badly the night before or has had a stressful weekend. We don't think through *alternative explanations*: we just assume that we're the problem.

Your mood is hardly likely to improve when you're thinking like this. It's like you're seeing the world through very badly focused glasses.

We've focused in this section on how our low mood influences the way we think, which then reinforces low mood. But in just the same way, when we're happy we generally think positive thoughts – which in turn strengthen our feelings of happiness. It's this kind of transformation that we want to help you achieve in this chapter.

Our behavior

Have a look back at the stories of Keith and Emily in Chapter 4. Their suspicious thoughts ended up makinsg them feel so low that neither of them wanted to leave the house. Social contact, whether it was going to work or socializing with friends, seemed too stressful. They did less and less, retreating into their homes and channelling all their energy into worrying.

Keith and Emily's cases show the way our behavior and mood are interconnected. When we're happy we're likely to be out and about, busy with work and hobbies and family and friends. These are just the sorts of behaviors and experiences that will keep our good mood going.

When we're feeling down, on the other hand, we're much more likely to do less. All of the activities that we used to do, including the ones we really enjoyed, now seem too difficult to face. Unfortunately, all this does is make us feel even more miserable and even less like doing things. After all, what we've done is remove from our lives the things that give us pleasure and a sense of achievement. Instead of feeling alive and involved in the world, we feel isolated and abandoned. No wonder we feel even lower than we did before.

Improving our mood

We've seen how our moods are the product of the way we think and the way we behave. So it stands to reason that *changing the way we think and behave will help us change our mood.* This is precisely what cognitive therapy sets out to achieve – and it's what we're going to show you how to do in the next few pages. Almost everyone, whatever their situation, will benefit from these techniques. But we particularly recommend them if you're feeling down and finding it hard to cope.

1 KEEP A RECORD OF HOW YOU'VE BEEN SPENDING YOUR TIME

Before you start making changes, you need to assess your current situation. Keep a diary for a week and focus on how you're spending your time rather than the way you're feeling. When the week is up, look back over your diary and see how much time you've spent doing the following:

- Socializing with friends;
- Being physically active;
- Doing things outdoors;
- Enjoying yourself;

- Keeping your mind active;
- Doing things that give you a sense of achievement;
- Sleeping;
- Being alone;
- Watching television;
- Being indoors;
- Doing stressful activities.

Think too about how well you've been eating and how much alcohol you've drunk.

Can you improve the way you spend your time? Can you add more *positive activity* to your week? That phrase 'positive activity' sounds a bit vague, but here are some examples:

- Being **physically** active: you could take part in a sport like swimming or running, do some gardening or just walk more.
- Being **mentally** active: try, for example, reading or doing a puzzle, learning a new skill or planning a project. You might want to join an evening class – it's a great way to boost your level of mental activity.
- Being **socially** active: spend more time with friends and family; go out more – perhaps to a restaurant or the cinema, or to watch a sport.

Have a think too about how you *manage* your time. Can you organize things so that you spend less time doing chores and more time doing the things you enjoy? And what about your diet? Can you eat more healthily? Can you cut back on your alcohol intake? Can you make your mealtimes more regular?

If you're anything like us, then there's probably room for improvement in most if not all of these areas. We're not asking you to transform yourself overnight into a model citizen. We know how hard it is to make these kinds of changes. But we would like you to add just *one* new positive activity to your week.

If you're finding it hard to think of a positive activity that's right for you, ask yourself the following questions:

- What could I do for an afternoon that I'd find really enjoyable or satisfying?
- What could I do for an hour?
- Is there something good I could plan to do one weekend?
- What can I do that costs money?
- What can I do for free?
- What could I do that will really stimulate my mind?
- What would give me a sense of achievement?
- Is there a course or evening class I'd find interesting?
- What physical activity would I like to do?

- What about learning some practical skill?
- If a friend was visiting what would I suggest we do?
- Do I want to meet new people?
- Do I want to make new friends?
- What enjoyable activity could I do on my own?
- What could I do at home?
- Where would I like to go?
- What could I do that I've never done before?
- What have I enjoyed doing in the past?
- Are there any interesting events or activities listed in the paper?
- How about voluntary work?

Once you've got some ideas about the activities you could do, weigh up their advantages and disadvantages. And don't for get to plan ahead. If you decide to do an evening class, for example, remember that'll you'll need to book in advance.

2 CHANGING THE WAY YOU THINK

We've seen already in this chapter how important the way we think is to the way we feel. If we're thinking negative thoughts we'll also *feel* negative about ourselves and the world.

To change a negative way of thinking you need to adopt exactly the same strategy we set out in Chapter 7 for dealing with suspicious thoughts. First, keep a record of your thoughts. Then you need to assess the thoughts, reviewing the evidence for and against them and deciding how convincing you find them. Last but not least, test out your negative thoughts. The more you understand your negative thoughts the better you'll be able to deal with them in the future – and the more likely it is that you'll be able to avoid them altogether.

Start by using the table below to keep a record of your negative thoughts over the course of a week. Negative thoughts are usually triggered by an event – for example, a difficult conversation. Start by noting the event. Then think about the relationship between your thoughts and your mood. If you begin to feel low see if you can remember what you were thinking. This exercise is all about tracking your negative thoughts but, if you're feeling happy, do you also notice a change in your thoughts?

At the end of the week have a look back at your thoughts and write down the evidence both for and against them. To help you do that ask yourself these questions:

- Is there anything that might suggest the thought could be wrong?
- What would my family or friends say if I talked to them about the thought?
- What would I say to a friend who came to me with a similar problem?
- If I believe the thought what's the effect on me?

- Are there any alternative explanations for what seems to have happened?
- Could I have reacted in a different way? How would I like to have reacted?

Day	Triggering event	Thoughts What went through your mind? What were you thinking about yourself, the world and the future?	Mood How did you feel?

Day	Thought Include a rating for how strongly you believed it (0–100%)	Evidence for	Evidence against Include alternative explanations – and show your compassion!	Rating How strongly do you believe the thought now?

When you're thinking about alternative explanations for events, or different reactions, try to show your 'inner compassion'. That's a phrase the psychologist Paul Gilbert uses. He points out that we're often very good at being supportive, sympathetic and sensitive to others, but much less effective in showing the same sort of compassion towards ourselves. We demand much more of ourselves than we do of others – and we're incredibly hard on ourselves when we don't live up to our impossibly high standards.

So go easy on yourself. Don't assume that everything's your fault. Remember that there are all sorts of explanation for every event – you can't be to blame for them all!

With that in mind assess your thoughts using the table opposite.

Finally, test out your negative thoughts – there's no better way to find out how reliable your thoughts are. Have a look back at Chapter 7 to remind yourself how we suggested you test your suspicious thoughts: it's just the same with negative thoughts. If you think someone's annoyed with you, go and ask them. If you think people don't want to socialize with you, invite them out. If you think you're a failure, start another pro ject and see how you get on.

We know this kind of thing is very hard. It can feel as if you're laying yourself open to rejection and humiliation. But the rewards you'll get will make it all worthwhile. You'll see that your negative thoughts are much more a reflection of the way you feel about yourself than they are of reality. Just as with suspicious thoughts, we mustn't fear our negative thoughts and we mustn't simply accept them. Instead, let's analyze, challenge and test them out.

Increasing your self-esteem

Where do negative thoughts come from? Our moods can play a part – when we're feeling down we tend to think negatively. But mainly they're a product of the way we view ourselves: our *self-esteem.*

Okay, so where does our self-esteem come from? Well, it's the product of our life experiences: the way we were brought up; our position in society and in the various groups we belong to (our families or school class, for instance); our interactions with other people; and the things that have happened to us.

Given the sheer number of influences involved it's not surprising that self-esteem is a complex thing. It's generally not possible to point to a single event in order to explain our self-esteem: it's the product of a combination of factors and it often changes over time.

That said, it's normally true that bad experiences lower our self-esteem and good ones raise it. And if we're not careful, we can get into another of those vicious circles: when we're feeling down, we ignore or dismiss positive experiences, which only reinforces our low self-esteem and, with it, our negative thoughts and low mood. If you'd like to know more about self-esteem and how cognitive therapy can help you might like to read Melanie Fennell's *Overcoming Low Self-Esteem* (see Further Reading).

If you're feeling down we want you to shift focus. There's a whole movement, Positive Psychology, which argues we have neglected the study and appreciation of happiness for too long. Now we want you to concentrate on the positive and really build your own happiness and self-esteem.

First, write down five positive qualities you think you have. For example, maybe you're generous, or supportive or friendly. Rate how strongly you believe each statement about yourself.

	Positive quality	Rating (0–100%)
1		
2		
3		
4		
5		

Now see if you can remember specific examples of these positive qualities. Close your eyes and visualize them as clearly as you can. Try to put yourself right back in the moment.

Next we want you to keep another diary. Just as you did first for suspicious thoughts and then for negative thoughts, keep a record of the positive things you do, or that happen to you, over the course of a week.

After you've kept the diary for a week have a look back at your list of positive qualities. Revisit the ratings and see whether you want to change any of them. Can you add any positive qualities to the list?

For many people this exercise helps them see the positive qualities they have, and notice the good things that happen to them. Don't feel you have to repeat the exercise over and over again, but do make sure you take regular time to think about the positive things in your life – the things you've done and the things that have happened to you.

Day	Positive thing you did or that happened to you	Mood (How did you feel?)

Learning to be more assertive

When our self-esteem is low, or when we're feeling down, we're often very reluctant to tell people what we want or need. Instead of expressing our feelings – for example, if someone's done something to upset us – we tend to shrink into the background and 'go with the flow'.

This *timidity* (or passiveness) stems from our fear about what might happen if we *do* express ourselves. Maybe we'll get into an argument, or the other person will think we're stupid. Maybe they'll just take no notice of us. If we say nothing we'll avoid any unpleasant confrontation, won't we?

Avoiding confrontation can make us feel better in the short term but the long-term consequences of timidity aren't so good. We come to see ourselves as weak and passive, always doing what other people want and never having the courage to stand up for our own needs and desires. Our self-esteem takes a real hit, and we can also feel a lot of resentment toward other people. In the end timidity makes us feel bad about both ourselves and the people around us. We're also not being fair: other people have a right to know if they're upsetting or annoying us.

We need to ditch our timidity and replace it with *assertiveness.* Assertiveness is really a recognition that other people aren't mind-readers. No one can know what we're thinking unless we tell them. So we need to *express ourselves* and let the people around us know how we feel and what we want. If you're not an assertive person right now, it can be hard to imagine that you ever will be. But assertiveness can definitely be learned and we'll give you some pointers in the next couple of pages.

By the way, assertiveness is sometimes confused with aggression. But it's not about getting what we want at all costs. We need to *respect* other people's feelings and remember that they, just like us, have needs and desires that deserve a fair hearing.

Okay, how do we go about being assertive? The first step is to be clear about what we want. If someone at work is making a joke at your expense, for example, you need to decide what you want to happen. Are you happy to let it go, or do you want this kind of thing to stop?

Let's say you've decided you want the joking to stop – what do you do next? You now need to tell the person concerned how you feel and what you want. Try to stay as cool and matter-of-fact as possible; in fact, if you've been really upset or angered by something that's happened it's a good idea to wait until you're feeling calmer before you have this conversation.

Make it very clear how you feel, but don't use extreme language like 'you always...' or 'you never...' Just concentrate on the incident at hand. Focus on the *effect* of the other person's behavior rather than what they may have been intending to achieve. You can't know for sure that the person in tended to upset you by telling that joke. But you do know how it made you feel – and that's what you should be explaining to them. You might say something like, 'I'm sure you didn't mean to, but that joke really upset me.'

Once you've communicated how you feel move on to what you want to happen. Again, make it as clear and specific as you can. Don't say you don't want them to upset you again: that's too vague. Tell them, 'I'd appreciate it if you didn't make these kinds of jokes about me in the future.'

Try to stay as calm and friendly as you can. No one responds positively when they feel they're under attack. If you go in with all guns blazing you'll probably just end up in a row. Bear in mind that most of us are very bad at judging how our behavior is seen by other people. You might well find that the person who made the joke had no idea of the effect it would have on you. They weren't being malicious, only thoughtless. And if you get a constructive response to your comments, remember to thank the other person for it.

One area where many people find it especially difficult to express their feelings is when they're asked to do something. We've all found ourselves loaded down with jobs we've no time or inclination to do simply because we find it impossible to say 'no'. Sometimes it's because we just want to be helpful. Sometimes it's because we're too scared of the consequences to say what we really think. Either way not being able to say 'no' isn't going to do much for our self-esteem. You can imagine how we'll feel about ourselves if the only thing preventing us from saying 'no' is fear. But even if we start out feeling good about ourselves for being so obliging, we'll probably end up feeling like we're really just too timid to stand up for ourselves.

Here are some techniques you can use to help you with that tiny but ever so tricky word:

• Buy yourself the time you need to be assertive (or if you're not sure how you feel about a task). When someone asks you to do something say you'll think about it.

• Don't make excuses and don't give reasons: just say no. For example, you could say 'No, I am sorry but I can't' or 'No, I can't do it this time' or just 'No, I'm sorry.' This is called the 'broken record' technique and is especially good for those situations where you're absolutely sure you don't want to do what you've been asked. Keeping your response this brief is a reflection of the fact that you don't need permission for your decision. You don't have to persuade anyone that your decision is the right one.

• Sometimes you'll want to show you appreciate being asked even though you're not able to help. So you might say, 'It's kind of you to ask me, but I can't' or 'Thanks for thinking of me, but I'd rather not.'

- Be sympathetic and constructive. Tell the person you see their problem and help them think through possible solutions – as long as they don't involve you, of course!
- Explain why you can't help. But don't fall into the trap of sounding as if you're making excuses. Remember: you have a valid reason for your decision and you don't need anyone's approval.
- Sometimes you might want to meet the other person halfway: 'I can't do x, but I may be able to help you with y.'

If you know you find it hard to be assertive in certain situations it's a good idea to plan ahead. Think of all the ways you could react in the future and then weigh up their pros and cons. Once you've decided on the best approach think through what you'd say. Visualize the situation as clearly as you can and re hearse your lines until you know them by heart. The more practice you do the easier it'll get. That said, we know that learning to be assertive can be hard, at least at first. It takes courage to speak up for yourself – and you should remember that when you do! Give yourself the praise you deserve.

Improving sleep

Many of the people we see at our clinic have sleep problems. Some find it very hard to get to sleep. Others don't sleep through the whole night.

Most of us have trouble sleeping once in a while. When it becomes persistent it's called *insomnia.* If you suffer from insomnia you're certainly not alone: it affects around 10 to 15 per cent of the population.

If you've experienced insomnia you won't need us to tell you how debilitating it can be. Most of us need seven to eight hours of sleep a night. If we don't get them it has a profound effect on the way we feel and function. Going without enough sleep is almost guaranteed to have a negative effect on our mood.

However, there is good news: there are some very effective techniques to beat insomnia. Let's look at them now. (For a more detailed discussion of insomnia and how CBT can help, see Colin Espie's *Overcoming Insomnia and Sleep Problems,* details in the Further Reading section.)

1 SLEEP HYGIENE

Getting the rest you need is partly about good *sleep hygiene.* By hygiene we don't of course mean scrubbing down your bedroom with disinfectant! We mean the key things you can do to improve your sleep.

• **Exercise every day.** We all know that exercise is good for our hearts and all-round health, but we often don't appreciate the great effect it has on our sleep. It's simple: exercise tires us out. And if we're tired, we're likely to sleep better. (Don't exe rcise late in the evening though: you'll just feel more awake.)

• **Cut out caffeine, alcohol and nicotine in the evening.** Caffeine and nicotine are stimulants which means they'll keep you awake. Alcohol is likely to make it easier to fall asleep, but there's a downside. Alcohol interferes with the natural stages of sleep. If you have drunk a lot you're also likely to wake up feeling thirsty or unwell. All in all you won't sleep as deeply or as long as you will if you haven't been drinking alcohol.

• **Develop a relaxing evening routine.** If you go straight to bed after being busy with something your mind will be buzzing with whatever it was you were doing. At least half an hour before bedtime begin winding down. Do something calm and relaxing: maybe a warm bath or some time reading or listening to gentle music.

• **Have a bedtime snack.** This one might seem a bit surprising, but a little bit of food about half an hour before bed can help with sleep. Make it something healthy and relatively plain: a glass of milk, a banana or maybe a piece of wholewheat toast. Don't eat too much: your body won't be able to rest if it's having to digest a meal.

• **Make your sleeping environment a good one.** You've probably discovered how difficult it is to sleep well if your bed is uncomfortable, if there's a lot of noise outside or if it's too light. Make sure your bedroom is set up with whatever you need for a good night's sleep.

2 SLEEP RULES

If your sleep hygiene is good but your insomnia isn't improving try following these sleep rules. They should make a positive difference after a few days.

- Cut out daytime naps – they will only make you feel less tired at night.
- Learn to associate your bed with sleep. We're creatures of habit. If you use your bed for all kinds of activities – reading, eating, watching TV, writing a diary – then your body will expect to be awake and alert when you go to bed. Instead, you need to train your body to start winding down for sleep the moment you get into bed. Do all those other things beforehand and use your bed only for sleep and sex.
- Only go to bed when you're tired.
- If you haven't fallen asleep within 20 minutes get up and do something else. Try to do something relaxing – listening to music or reading a book. It's the same if you wake up in the night: if you haven't fallen back to sleep after 20 minutes, get up and only go back to bed when you're feeling tired.

• Don't lie in. This doesn't sound much fun, but it's important to get up at the same time each morning rather than trying to catch up on sleep.

• Many people find they're kept awake by worrying. If this happens to you use the worry periods technique we de scribed in Chapter 8. Let go of your worries for now and deal with them in your next worry period.

When you start your new regime of only going to bed when you're tired and getting up at the same time every morning, you might well find yourself feeling sleepy during the day. That's fine: it's a sign that your body is adjusting to the changes. Don't give into the temptation to have a nap in the day or go to bed really early. If you're tired at your normal bedtime that's great: it will help you get to sleep. Within a few days you'll find that your body has got used to your new sleep pattern – and your sleeping will be all the better for it.

***

This chapter has been all about helping you to feel happy and well. We can all benefit from the key messages about improving our mood, raising our self-esteem, being more assertive and making sure we eat and sleep well. But if you're having problems with suspicious thoughts they can make an especially big difference. To put it in a nutshell: *feeling better about yourself means you're much less likely to have paranoid thoughts.*

If you've made it all the way through this book, and especially if you've tried the exercises we've suggested, you can feel rightly proud of your efforts. We hope you will now have a much greater understanding of suspicious thoughts: where they come from, why they can cause so much distress and – most importantly – how they can be beaten.

Now might be a good time to revisit the exercises in Step 1 in Chapter 6. They will help you assess what your experience of suspicious thoughts is like now – and of course we hope you'll see that it's much improved from when you started this book.

If you want to know more about the issues we've discussed in this book, or if you feel you'd like more help, check out the information in the Appendix.

CHAPTER SUMMARY

• Improving the way we feel about ourselves and the world – our **mood** – will help reduce the number of suspicious thoughts we have.

• One very effective way of improving our mood is by **building a happy and healthy lifestyle.**

• Increase the number of **positive activities** in your life. Keep busy with things you find enjoyable and rewarding.

- Analyze, challenge and test out your negative thoughts.
- Raise your self-esteem by acknowledging your **positive qualities** and the good things in your life.
- Learn to be **more assertive.**
- Sleep well!

Appendix

Getting more help: Therapists and medication

This book is all about helping you cope with your suspicious thoughts. You will know the trouble and distress these thoughts can cause, but by now we hope you will also have seen how you can put them behind you and get on with the rest of your life.

If you are still having problems with paranoid thoughts after having worked with this book you may feel you want to consider other sources of help – perhaps seeing a therapist or trying medication. Or you might just want to find out a bit more about the issues. In this Appendix we set out the options for additional help.

Professional help

You will probably have grown tired by now of our reminder that everyone experiences suspicious thoughts from time to time. However, only a small proportion of us ever see a doctor about them so how do we know when it's right to ask for professional help?

There is no easy answer to this one, but basically it comes down to:

- How distressing you're finding the thoughts
- How much they're disrupting your life.

If the thoughts are making you feel very anxious or down, or if they're stopping you from functioning as you'd like to, then you may well want to think about seeking professional help. You should definitely do so if you're feeling very depressed or even suicidal.

That said, even if your suspicious thoughts aren't having an especially severe effect, they can still be unsettling. Even if you feel you are coping, you might nonetheless find it helpful to talk things over with your doctor, see a therapist or try out some medication. You may also want a doctor to check to see whether your suspicious thoughts might be caused by one of the medical conditions we mentioned in Chapter 2 (in section entitled "Medical and psychiatric conditions").

Sometimes we're just too close to the situation to know whether or not we need help. Talk things over with trusted friends or relatives: they will be able to give their perspective on how your paranoid thoughts are affecting you.

If you do decide to seek professional help it's crucial that you find the right person. If you think your doctor doesn't understand paranoid thoughts and their treatment, ask to be referred to a specialist. It is relatively easy to get knowledgeable advice on medication, but harder to find someone with specialist psychological knowledge – however, the information in this Appendix should help.

Cognitive Behavior Therapy (CBT)

There are lots of types of psychological therapy (also called 'psychotherapy' or 'talking therapy'). But the therapy that has been proved to be highly effective in dealing with suspicious thoughts – and the one that we draw upon throughout this book – is *Cognitive Behavior Therapy* (or CBT for short).

Cognitive Behavioral Therapy is a *collaborative* therapy. You and your therapist will work together to:

- Agree the goals of the therapy;
- Identify the causes of your distress;
- Decide on strategies for reducing that distress.

You can expect the therapist to share their knowledge with you and to regularly monitor your progress, but it's definitely *not* a case of the therapist simply telling you what the problem is and what you should do about it.

How many sessions of CBT will you need? Well, that's something you will work out with your therapist but most people have around ten to twenty weekly sessions. You can expect the therapy to draw on the sorts of strategies and thinking we pre sent in this book, but there are other benefits. For a start, most people find that having the opportunity to discuss their pro blems with a sympathetic and knowledge-able person is a real positive. The structure of weekly appointments can also really boost your mo-tivation and your therapist will be able to help you with the exercises and may well spot things of which you're unaware. He or she will also be able to help with other problems you may have.

CBT therapists

Cognitive Behavioral Therapy is mainly provided by clinical psychologists, although more and more psychiatrists, counsel ling psychologists, counsellors and nurses are becoming trained in this approach.

Clinical psychologists have studied psychology at university and then completed a three-year postgrad-uate degree. Most also have a doctoral degree in clinical psychology (meaning that they use the word 'Doctor' before their name). Clinical psychologists apply psychological theories and research to prob-lems and do not prescribe medication.

Psychiatrists have trained as medical doctors and then gone on to specialize in the care of people with mental health problems. Their first line of treatment is usually medication, but some psychiatrists are also trained in psychological therapies such as CBT. Defining the term *counsellor* is more difficult. It is a title used by people with widely differing types and amounts of training. Chartered counselling psycholo-gists, for example, have studied for several years, obtained a doctoral degree and are often very similar to clinical psychologists. Some counsellors have extensive training but not in CBT. Others have only attended short courses. When you are looking for a counsellor check that they have been properly trained, that they are a specialist in CBT and that they belong to an appropriate professional body. A number of organizations keep registers of CBT therapists (for example, the British Association for Behavioral and Cognitive Psychotherapies) and you can find details of these in the list of useful organizations.

Getting CBT

If you want to explore the options for getting CBT it's usually best to talk first to your family doctor. Your doctor has a good general knowledge of common illnesses and will be able to advise you on access to local resources and refer you to a therapist if appropriate. It is important that you are referred to a therapist who has been properly trained in the use of CBT: ask your doctor if you're not sure.

In the UK most CBT therapists work in the National Health Service. Alternatively you may want to consider seeing a private therapist. Sometimes private therapy can be arranged by your family doctor. If not, you may need to find a therapist on your own. As ever, make sure your therapist is properly qualified. (Again, see the list of useful organizations for help with this.)

Medication

Medication is often prescribed for people who are suffering with severe paranoid thoughts and many of them find it helps. Remember that psychologists and counsellors can't prescribe medication; only family doctors and psychiatrists can do so. As part of the consultation they will want to investigate possible physical causes of the suspicious thoughts. For example, they may take a blood sample so they can check for infection and see how your liver, kidneys and thyroid gland are functioning.

Two major categories of medication are given to combat paranoid thoughts:

- Neuroleptics;
- Anti-depressants.

Each of these two categories (which we'll discuss in more detail below) includes lots of different individual drugs. Fin ding out about these drugs can be a confusing business because they all have at least two names. Each drug has an official medical name (its *generic* name) and the *trade* name given by the company that makes it. For example, the drug fluoxetine is widely known by the trade name Prozac. We use the generic names in this Appendix.

Everyone responds differently to particular drugs so it may take time to find the right medication and the right dose. Each drug also has its own set of potential side-effects and risks. Your doctor will discuss with you how you're getting on with the medication prescribed and he or she may alter the dose or even the drug until you find the one that's most effective. Make sure your doctor explains:

• How much of the medication to take and how often;
• The potential side-effects;
• How you would go about stopping the medication, if that's what you eventually decide (for example, it's usually best to gradually reduce the amount you take rather than immediately stopping altogether).

Neuroleptics

As we've mentioned neuroleptics are one of the two major types of drug prescribed for suspicious thoughts. They are sometimes called 'anti-psychotics' or 'major tranquillizers'. Neuroleptics are mainly prescribed for people with mental health problems such as schizophrenia or psychosis, but in smaller doses they are sometimes used to treat anxiety and agitation.

Neuroleptics take a few days or weeks to act. If one doesn't work doctors often try one of the others. There are lots of neuroleptic medications now. The older ones in-clude chlorpromazine, haloperidol and trifluoperazine. Among the newer ones, often called 'atypical neuroleptics', are risperidone, amisulpride, olanzepine and clozapine. If your doctor suggests a neuroleptic it's likely to be a low dose of an atypical.

The downside of neuroleptics is the unpleasant and occasionally severe side-effects they can produce including drowsiness, weight gain, reduced sexual desire and diabetes.

Anti-depressants

Your doctor may feel that your suspicious thoughts will reduce if your mood is better. In this case he or she will probably prescribe an anti-depressant. There are various types of anti-depressants, but it's most likely you would be given one of the newer *SSRIs* (or 'selective serotonin reuptake inhibitors').

Commonly used SSRIs are fluoxetine, paroxetine, citalopram and sertraline. As with neuroleptics, it may be a while before the SSRI starts working. However, the side-effects (for example, stomach upset, agita-tion, rashes, reduced sexual desire) are usually less common and less severe than those caused by neu-roleptics.

The other commonly prescribed type of anti-depres-sants is the *tricyclics* – examples include amitriptyline, imipramine and clomipramine. SSRIs are thought to have fewer side-effects than the tricyclic medications.

The Web site www.mentalhealthcare.org.uk offers you the chance to post questions about medication to the Maudsley Hospital Chief Pharmacist. The Maudsley Hospital also runs a Mental Health Medication Helpline (Tel. No. 020 7919 2999, weekdays 11a.m.–5p.m.).

Further reading

This is the only self-help guide dealing with suspicious thoughts, though you may be interested in *Paranoia: The Twenty-first Century Fear* by Daniel Freeman and Jason Freeman (Oxford University Press, 2008), which is a concise and accessible look at the prevalence and causes of paranoia in contemporary society. There are also many excellent books on related topics and we list some of these below. Many of the Overcoming titles are recommended on the NHS Books on Prescription Scheme. However, don't feel restricted to our suggestions: take the time to browse in a good bookshop or library and select the book you find the most readable and helpful. Alter natively, online stores such as Amazon stock hundreds of self-help titles.

Anxiety

Overcoming Anxiety, Helen Kennerley (Robinson, 1997).

Overcoming Anxiety, Chris Williams (Hodder & Arnold, 2003).

Overcoming Panic, Derek Silove and Vuaya Manicavasagar (Robinson, 1997).

Overcoming Social Anxiety and Shyness, Gillian Butler (Robinson, 1999).

Panic Attacks, Christine Ingham (HarperCollins, 2000).

Assertiveness

Assert Yourself, Gael Lindenfield (HarperCollins, 2001).

Depression

Feeling Good, David Burns (Avon Books, 2000).

Mind Over Mood, Dennis Greenberger and Christine Padesky (Guilford Press, 1995).

Overcoming Depression, Paul Gilbert (Robinson, 2000).

Overcoming Depression, Chris Williams (Hodder & Arnold, 2001).

Insomnia

Overcoming Insomnia and Sleep Problems, Colin Espie (Robinson, 2006).

Mental Health

Manage Your Mind: The Mental Fitness Guide, Gillian Butler and Tony Hope (Oxford Paperbacks, 1995).

Staying Sane: How To Make Your Mind Work for You, Raj Persaud (Bantam, 2001).

Post-traumatic Stress Disorder

I Can't Get Over It: Handbook for Trauma Survivors, Aphrodite Matsakis (New Harbinger, 1996).

Overcoming Traumatic Stress, Claudia Herbert and Ann Wetmore (Robinson, 1999).

Relationships

Love is Never Enough: How Couples Can Overcome Misunder standings, Resolve Conflicts, and Solve Relationship Problems Thro ugh Cognitive Therapy, Aaron Beck (HarperCollins, 1989).

Over coming Relationship Problems, Michael Crowe (Robinson, 2005)

Schizophrenia

Coping with Schizophrenia: A Guide for Patients, Families and Caregivers, Steven Jones and Peter Hayward (One World, 2004).

Living with Mental Illness: A Book for Relatives and Friends, Elizabeth Kuipers and Paul Bebbington (Souvenir Press, 2004).

Recent Advances in Understanding Mental Illness and Psychotic Experiences, British Psychological Society (BPS, 2000). This can be downloaded at: www.understandingpsychosis.com

The Complete Family Guide to Schizophrenia: Helping Your Loved One Get the Most Out of Life, Kim T. Mueser and Susan Gingerich (Guildford Press, 2006).

Self-esteem

Overcoming Low Self-Esteem, Melanie Fennell (Robinson, 1999).

10 Days to Great Self-Esteem, David Burns (Vermilion, 2000).

Stress Management

Managing Stress, Terry Looker and Olga Gregson (Teach Your self Books, 2003).

Stress Management for Dummies, Allen Elkin (Hungry Minds, 1999).

If you would like to provide feedback on *Overcoming Paranoid and Suspicious Thoughts* or would like to share your experiences with others, visit: www.para noidthoughts.com.

Useful organizations

A number of health profession organizations and mental health charities provide information and support. Some of them also keep registers of cognitive therapists (though being listed doesn't mean a particular therapist is a specialist in suspicious thoughts). We list the organizations within a country alphabetically.

UK

British Association for Behavioural and Cognitive Psychotherapies
Victoria Buildings
9-13 Silver Street
Bury
BL9 0EU
Tel: +44 (0)161 7974484
Fax: +44 (0)161 7972670
Email: > babcp@babcp.com
www.babcp.com
Lists accredited cognitive therapists.

British Psychological Society
St. Andrews House
48 Princess Road East
Leicester
LE1 7DR
Tel.:+44 (0)116 254 9568

Web site: www.bps.org.uk
Email: enquiry@bps.org.uk
Lists chartered clinical psychologists.

The Mental Health Foundation

9th Floor
Sea Containers House
20 Upper Ground
London
SE1 9QB
Tel.: +44 (0)20 7803 1100
Web site: www.mentalhealth.org.uk

MIND (National Association for Mental Health)

15–19 Broadway
London
E15 4BQ
Tel.: +44 (0)20 8519 2122
Information line: +44 (0)845 766 0163
Web site: www.mind.org.uk
Email: contact@mind.org.uk

Oxford Cognitive Therapy Centre

Psychology Department
Warneford Hospital
Oxford
OX3 7JX
Tel.: +44 (0)1865 223986
Web site: www.octc.co.uk

Rethink
5th Floor
Royal London House
22–25 Finsbury Square
London
EC2A 1DX
Rethink general enquiries:
Tel.: +44 (0)845 456 0455 or email: info@rethin
 k.org
National Advice service:
Tel.: +44 (0)20 8974 6814 or email: advice@ret
 hink.org
Web site: www.rethink.org

The Royal College of Psychiatrists
17 Belgrave Square
London
SW1X 8PG
Tel.: +44 (0)20 7235 2351
Web site: www.rcpsych.ac.uk
Email: rcpsych@rcpsych.ac.uk

SANE
1st Floor
Cityside House
40 Adler Street
London
E1 1EE
Tel.: +44 (0)20 7375 1002
SANELINE (helpline): +44 (0)845 767 8000

Web site: www.sane.org.uk

The South London and Maudsley NHS Trust/Institute of Psychiatry, King's College London

The Maudsley Hospital
Denmark Hill
London
SE5 8AZ
Web sites: www.iop.kcl.ac.uk
www.slam.nhs.uk
www.mentalhealthcare.org.uk
Mental Health Medication Helpline: +44 (0)20 7919 2999

The Trust's PICuP Clinic provides CBT for severe paranoia, although referrals have to be from a community mental health team. The PICuP Clinic (Psychological Intervention Clinic for Outpatients with Psychosis) can be contacted on: Tel.: 020 7919 3524. Email: picup@iop.kcl.ac.uk

EUROPE

The European Association for Behavioural and Cognitive Psychotherapies (EABCT) Web site (www.eabct.com) provides links to national cognitive therapy organizations in Europe. It lists, for example, the Web site for the Netherlands Association of Behaviour and Cognitive Therapy (which keeps a register of cognitive therapists): www.vgct.nl

USA

The Academy of Cognitive Therapy
1 Belmont Avenue
Suite 700
Bala Cynwyd
PA 19004-1610
Tel.: (610) 664-1273
Fax: (610) 664-5137
Web site: www.academyofct.org
Email: info@academyofct.org
*Lists accredited cognitive therapists in the US and
other countries.*

American Psychiatric Association
1000 Wilson Boulevard
Suite 1825
Arlington
VA 22209–3901
APA Answer Centre: 1-888-35-PSYCH
From outside the USA and Canada, tel:
 001-703-907-7300
Web site: www.psych.org
Email: apa@psych.org

American Psychological Society
750 First Street
NE, Washington
DC 20002-4242
Tel: (800) 374-2721 or (202) 336-5500

Web site: www.apa.org
Keeps a register of psychologists.

Association for Behavioral and Cognitive Therapies (ABCT)

305 Seventh Avenue – 16th Floor
New York
NY 10001-6008
Tel.: (212) 647-1890 Web site:
www.aabt.org
Keeps a directory of cognitive and behavior therapists.

Beck Institute for Cognitive Therapy and

Research
One Belmont Avenue, Suite 700
Bala Cynwyd
PA 19004-1610
Tel: (610) 664-3020
Web site: www.beckinstitute.org

National Alliance for the Mentally Ill (NAMI)

Colonial Place Three
2107 Wilson Blvd, Suite 300
Arlington
VA 22201-3042
Information Helpline: 1-800-950-NAMI (6264)
Web site: www.nami.org

National Institute of Mental Health

Public Information and Communications Branch

6001 Executive Boulevard, Room 8184, MSC 9663
Bethesda
MD 20892–9663
Tel: 301-443-4513 (local)
1-866-615-6464 (toll-free)
Web site: www.nimh.nih.gov
Email: nimhinfo@nih.gov

National Mental Health Association (NMHA)

National Mental Health Association
2000 N. Beauregard Street, 6th Floor
Alexandria
Virginia 22311
Tel.: (703) 684-7722
Web site: www.nmha.org

Title
Overcoming Anger and Irritability
Overcoming Anorexia Nervosa
Overcoming Anxiety
Overcoming Anxiety Self-Help Course (3 parts)
Overcoming Bulimia Nervosa and Binge-Eating Self-Help Course (3 parts)
Overcoming Childhood Trauma
Overcoming Chronic Fatigue
Overcoming Chronic Pain
Overcoming Compulsive Gambling
Overcoming Depersonalizaton and Feelings of Unreality
Overcoming Depression
Overcoming Depression: Talks With Your Therapist (Audio)
Overcoming Grief
Overcoming Insomnia and Sleep Problems
Overcoming Low Self-Esteem
Overcoming Low Self-Esteem Self-Help Course (3 parts)
Overcoming Mood Swings
Overcoming Obsessive Compulsive Disorder
Overcoming Panic
Overcoming Panic and Agoraphobia Self-Help Course (3 parts)
Overcoming Paranoid and Suspicious Thoughts
Overcoming Problem Drinking
Overcoming Relationship Problems
Overcoming Sexual Problems

Title
Overcoming Social Anxiety and Shyness
Overcoming Social Anxiety and Shyness Self-Help Course (3 parts)
Overcoming Traumatic Stress
Overcoming Weight Problems
Overcoming Worry
Overcoming Your Child's Fears and Worries
Overcoming Your Child's Shyness and Social Anxiety
Overcoming Your Smoking Habit
Manage Your Mood: Behavioral Techniques to Overcome Deppresion

Name: _____
Address: _____
Postcode: _____
Daytime Tel No: _____
Email: _____
(in case of query)

How to Pay:

1. **By telephone:** call the TBS order line on 01206 255 800 and quote PET. Phone lines are open between Monday–Friday, 8.30am–5.30pm.

2. **By post:** send a cheque for the full amount payable to TBS Ltd, or if paying by debit, credit or Switch card, fill in the details above and send the form to: Freepost RLUL-SJGC-SGKJ. Cash

Sales/Direct Mail Dept, The Book Service, Colchester Road, Frating, Colchester, CO7 7DW

Constable & Robinson Ltd (directly or via its agents) may mail or phone you about promotions or products Tick if you do not want these from us _ or our subsidiaries_

Books For ALL Kinds of Readers

At ReadHowYouWant we understand that one size does not fit all types of readers. Our innovative, patent pending technology allows us to design new formats to make reading easier and more enjoyable for you. This helps improve your speed of reading and your comprehension. Our EasyRead printed books have been optimized to improve word recognition, ease eye tracking by adjusting word and line spacing as well as minimizing hyphenation. Our EasyRead SuperLarge editions have been developed to make reading easier and more accessible for vision-impaired readers. We offer Braille and DAISY formats of our books and all popular E-Book formats.

We are continually introducing new formats based upon research and reader preferences. Visit our web-site to see all of our formats and learn how you can Personalize our books for yourself or as gifts. Sign up to Become A RHYW Registered Reader.

www.readhowyouwant.com

Made in the USA
Coppell, TX
23 April 2020